FOUND ARCHITECTURE

Sinéad Morrissey was born in Northern Ireland in 1972 and educated at Trinity College, Dublin. Her awards include a Lannan Literary Fellowship (2007), First Prize in the UK National Poetry Competition (2007), the *Irish Times* Poetry Now Award (2009, 2013) and the T.S. Eliot Prize (2013). In 2016 she received the E.M. Forster Award from the American Academy of Arts and Letters. *On Balance* was awarded the Forward Prize in 2017. She was elected a Fellow of the Royal Society of Literature in 2019. She has served as Belfast Poet Laureate (2013–14) and is currently Professor of Creative Writing at Newcastle University.

Also by Sinéad Morrissey

On Balance
Parallax
Through the Square Window
The State of the Prisons
Between Here and There
There Was Fire in Vancouver

SINÉAD MORRISSEY

Found Architecture

SELECTED POEMS

CARCANET

First published in Great Britain in 2020 by
Carcanet
Alliance House, 30 Cross Street
Manchester M2 7AQ
www.carcanet.co.uk

A CIP catalogue record for this book is
available from the British Library.
ISBN 978 1 78410 931 8

Book design by Andrew Latimer
Printed in Great Britain by SRP Ltd, Exeter, Devon

The publisher acknowledges financial
assistance from Arts Council England.

CONTENTS

from There Was Fire in Vancouver (1996)

from Between Here and There (2002)

from Parallax (2013)

from On Balance (2017)

FOUND ARCHITECTURE

for my family

from THERE WAS FIRE IN VANCOUVER (1996)

I remember smoke and faces that I knew
and the fact that I got in free; my mother
taking money by the half-collapsed sink;
posters proclaiming AN EVENING OF BRECHT
and subtitled *Bring Your Own Drink;*
too much conviction to see through.

CND

I want to grow up, not blow up! –
my slogan balloon and my CND badge
and my grin on the front of the *Belfast Telegraph*.
Nine years old and filled to the brim
with my parents' demands for peace.

The Trade Union Congress on Fallout
stretched through Saturday.
Between a windowless Bangor and a melting city
I signed hate mail to Reagan,
collected stickers, tasted beer.

It wasn't until I saw two skeletons,
scared of the sky, of the hole in the high-rise,
that it began to mean tears.
The still fear of being nothing too soon and too suddenly
silenced me for the day.

EUROPA HOTEL

It's a hard truth to have to take in the face –
you wake up one morning with your windows
round your ankles and your forehead billowing smoke;
your view impaired for another fortnight
of the green hills they shatter you for.

AWAITING BURIAL

Being born was as painful as this –
the crusade of the heart to bloom in mist,

the pull of blood
on everything the body had

to pump in a new direction,
the sliding dissection

of water
and air –

getting the heart to falter
and the lungs to breathe water

requires
the tonweight of the sky,

a damaged hillside, night-time,
the tunnel you dreamt of, O

Sarah, speak to me, you've been through
the journey, was there light on the other side

LEAVING FLENSBURG

This city settled on you in layers of days
that brought a grounding with them, that sense of knowing
where your feet belonged. Memory built the way
in which you recognised the place, decided how much your going
would cost: a few confused days in the next stop-over, or dreamscape
    for a year.

This one was a hard one to guess, because although
your feet knew all the town's directions,
and tapped their way through the map they'd got to know,
they never saw their own reflection
in the Baltic harbour: the thousand jellyfish that swarm in
    in September

made the glass shiver and the sky disappear.
All the same, you had the Glücksburg Autumn, days when the gold
set loose in the sky seemed almost like a crime. You feared
the winter, but it came, and the darkness and cold
brought with them skies of stars, high over Schleswig-Holstein, singing
    in space.

Above all, the shipyard rocketed the price –
freezing and full of sad men welding steel. It was almost dark
as the finished freighter slid out to the sea, and the thin ice
cracked in the shapes of flowers, all the way to Denmark.
It was then you knew there'd be dreams for years.

LOSING A DIARY

I

Semi-ship-wrecked in the harbour at Howth,
the fishing trawler (or cargo boat,
or one man's lifelong retirement dream proved excessive,
washed up and rusted) skulked in the sun.
The radio was on in the bridge but no one listened.
Tied down to everything it was and wasn't,
the whole crate bobbed and creaked. On the prow
stood a two-litre carton of milk, sliced
neatly in half, and full of old rain water.

II

Losing a diary is losing a line to the harbour.
I enter the past in open sea, leave in storm
and none of what I visit can be moored or married
to the sad, fixed honesty of how it was.

THERE WAS FIRE IN VANCOUVER

There was fire in Vancouver,
and we leaned out into the night to watch it
set light to the East End.
It had taken stand on Commercial Avenue.

We marvelled at the darkness of the city,
all neon dulled by the superior flame,
and wondered would it bestow its dance
on the Ginseng Teahouse in Chinatown, on Jericho Pier.

There were no sirens, hoses, buckets even,
scattering streets and 'Fire!' 'Fire!'
we seemed the only ones conscious of the bright crusade
and we watched with Moses standing in our heads.

from BETWEEN HERE AND THERE (2002)

IN BELFAST

I

Here the seagulls stay in off the Lough all day.
Victoria Regina steering the ship of the City Hall
in this the first and last of her intense provinces,
a ballast of copper and gravitas.

The inhaling shop-fronts exhale the length
and breadth of Royal Avenue, pause,
inhale again. The city is making money
on a weather-mangled Tuesday.

While the house for the Transport Workers' Union
fights the weight of the sky and manages
to stay up, under the Albert Bridge the river
is simmering at low tide and sheeted with silt.

11

I have returned after ten years to a corner
and tell myself it is as real to sleep here
as the twenty other corners I have slept in.
More real, even, with this history's dent and fracture

splitting the atmosphere. And what I have been given
is a delicate unravelling of wishes
that leaves the future unspoken and the past
unencountered and unaccounted for.

This city weaves itself so intimately
it is hard to see, despite the tenacity of the river
and the iron sky; and in its downpour and its vapour I am
as much at home here as I will ever be.

TOURISM

Like the relief of markets,
their saffron-coloured cloths and carpets,
purification where two rivers cross, or the widening line of light
entering Newgrange on the winter solstice –

a manufactured prophesy of spring –
the Spanish and the Dutch are landing in airports
and filing out of ships. Our day has come.

They bring us deliverance, restitution,
as we straighten our ties, strengthen our lattés,
polish our teeth. We take them to those streets
they want to see most, at first,

as though it's all over and safe behind bus glass
like a staked African wasp. Unabashedly, this is our splintered city,
and this, the corrugated line between doorstep and headstone.

Next, fearing summary,
we buy them a pint with a Bushmills chaser
and then on to the festering gap in the shipyard
the Titanic made when it sank.

Our talent for holes that are bigger
than the things themselves
resurfaces at Stormont, our weak-kneed parliament,

which, unlike Rome, we gained in a day
and then lost, spectacularly, several days later
in a shower of badly played cards. Another instance, we say,
of our off-beat, headstrong, suicidal charm.

So come, keep coming here.
We'll recklessly set chairs in the streets and pray for the sun.
Diffuse the gene pool, confuse the local kings,

infect us with your radical ideas; be carried here
on a sea breeze from the European Superstate
we long to join; bring us new symbols,
a new national flag, a xylophone. Stay.

& FORGIVE US OUR TRESPASSES

Of which the first is love. The sad, unrepeatable fact
that the loves we shouldn't foster burrow faster and linger longer
than sanctioned kinds can. Loves that thrive on absence, on lack
of return, or worse, on harm, are unkillable, Father.
They do not die in us. And you know how we've tried.
Loves nursed, inexplicably, on thoughts of sex,
a return to touched places, a backwards glance, a sigh –
they come back like the tide. They are with us at the terminus
when cancer catches us. They have never been away.
Forgive us the people we love – their dragnet influence.
Those disallowed to us, those who frighten us, those who stay
on uninvited in our lives and every night revisit us.
Accept from us the inappropriate
by which our dreams and daily scenes stay separate.

IN NEED OF A FUNERAL

Even though no one has died and there is no one
to touch in the coffin the way my brother
touched the dead-man relation
whose name we didn't know, whose features furrowed
like set sugar and whose black nails shone –
I have need of a funeral.

Even though death is not where I wish to go to,
down the wet green road through the straight black gate –
I have love in the morning, a candle, a radio
and a child's smile blooms over my fireplace.
If I don't walk to the river the river is by my window –
I have need of a funeral.

It came to me the day I stole communion in the cathedral,
not knowing what to do and squinting wildly,
that I had need of a funeral.
Something the man said as he tipped wine
and crushed bread felt helpful. He said sometimes a line
between what was and what is can be visible,

which is why we eat flesh and drink blood. *Kirie.*
I took flowers, an Oxfam veil, a bottle of Scotch, a speech
and made it to the sprawl of Milltown Cemetery
where I littered a hill with old shoes and milk teeth.

There was a pattern to the pattern my breath made on the air
as it extended towards the motorway.

ROCK POOL

These creatures live on faith that the greater sea,
whose roaring pounds and permeates the rock pool's floor,
the rock pool's leather-bound sanctuary, will once again rise up
to the little sea and that their salts will mingle and hold.
My arm submerged is a Eucalyptus tree
in an eighteenth-century birthing room, lurid and luminous.

How the women who have blocked the keyholes
and the door jams with rags and snuffed the candles scurry!
They move as suddenly as the travelling specks of eyes
that haunt vision: one look at them and they're gone
but they still look on. Water pours from the raised fringe
of green gauze like generosity. The pool collects itself again.

These creatures have lodged themselves on the tallest ridge
of the law of averages, the law of probability, and on the memory
of what their ancestors learned and saw, as unswayably
as they swell in crevices and suck rocks. Life flourishes on belief –
it announces quietly how, some day or night, the sea will arrive and save
     them
from the starfish-seeking children and evaporation.

How they would shine in a parable on the return of Christ.
How they would give women succour, those who also hang on
for the moon to peak and for water to answer. A stick breaks but does
     not break
as it enters the mirror. When I bend to the surface the room underwater
clouds and furrows with breath like a door closing over.
I am not theirs and they will not give me up.

STITCHES

There has been extravagance in speech
and every spilled, exploded word has been a stitch
in a blanket made for an imaginary baby.
The words went south where the sun was, but stayed hungry.

A name came in the third month. A face followed.
A hair type, a footprint, but the stitches showed.
Imagination's cloth too coarsely woven
for life to catch and cover stitching over.

And then blood. Inevitable, true.
Simple and strong enough to cut all falsehood through.
Later the screen said darkness – no spine, no heart.
And the stitches came apart.

We found ambition caked around his heart,
    hard as permafrost. Slowly
        we unpacked it, chipping it
block by block into a bucket. It was crude and unforgiving,
    like cement, and came away from the bone
        in white quartz chunks.
He had them fooled. They never guessed in all his airy silence
    how tuned to the pulse of the world he was.
        Arteries were stretched
where his first thirst had widened them, purple
    where the bruises of expansion had formed
        but still, away from the heart stem,
thin. His system pumped ambition till it killed him.

Both kidneys were filled with the by-product of not speaking:
    a viscous residue, yellow where the light had spilled
        into the incision, visibly oxidising.

We found his gifts, variously coloured or stored in variously-
    coloured liquids. His perfect pitch
        a perfect indigo, borrowed from a rainbow,
under an armpit. The lilac sac floating his liver, an impression of peace.
    His third eye lay buried in the pleura of the lungs
        where dreams of the violently deceased
had left their mark in larkspur and magenta. Out of the throat
    we prised a throat stone –
        originally cream, but shaded grey in places
with pain; the stunning span of his vocabulary worn to a solid entity
    by being understated.

He must, at times, have craved amnesia from impressions.
      Meninges cupping the brain were blue –
            the tell-tale print of synesthesia –
and so he tasted shapes, saw orchestral refrains as phantasmagoria,
      but also heard streetlights screaming
            and couldn't sleep in cities. Sir,
the deceased was overly gifted, oppressively bright,
      burdened with experience, psychically aware.
            His silence was the immovable object
the weight of all his talent solidified against. He should be kept
      in a crypt, open to the public, like Lenin is,
            and visited, to prove what sense is.

JO GRAVIS IN HIS METAL GARDEN

From the window of the midnight-bound Vegas plane
Tucson flares in the desert – a cactus pricked by rain;
lit houses, lit highways and floodlit swimming pools –
a stunned bird in a basin, spreading its wings to cool.
The gaudiness of Winterhaven is visible from air
in the aftermath of Christmas. Down in the dazzle somewhere
Jo Gravis is sleeping in his metal garden. It took a year
of free time strung like stepping stones from hour to hour
to finally clear his yard of rocks and the herbs he grew
as a solitary failed commercial venture – ginseng and feverfew.
Each hour of work an island. As though delivering his heart
from alcohol, he struck down to the bedrock of a humble start
and stood there a long time, exposed and rarified. At first,
he simply let the pictures come, withstood the thirst
and suffered the parade of soldiers, beggars, widows, orphans,
owls without trees and waterless swans and dolphins
until a gate latched in his mind and he had them forever.
He knew then he could commit them to metal to challenge the weather
and started to build. Metal the medium and metal the message,
he turned trolleys into children, knives into rose petals
from the pockets of Juan Diego, miraculous, crimson,
a velvet gift of proof from a virgin in a vision
hardened against the sun. He peeled flesh back from the bone
and fooled no one. When his women with aerial hair were done
his kettle-headed men stood guard against them by a river
of headlights and bicycle wheels. Such honesty in silver
puts constancy in a peeled hand of wires against the sky
and hope in a speechless sort of prophecy –
a teddy bear bound with twine to an orange tree,
its eyes replaced with pearls. With all of these images
hard and permanent and real and safe in cages

Jo Gravis sensed a sweet deliverance, an end to motion, and finally built himself a wooden bench to sleep on surrounded by signs – their shadows on his skin a lullaby to flesh in a fleshless gallery.

THIS CENTURY, THE NEXT, THE LAST

My husband requests a sky burial
he wishes to be
as carrion sequestered by leopards
strung up in a desert tree

Back to the familiar corridor he
may choose any opening
but all the rooms contain me
dressed for a wedding

AN ANATOMY OF SMELL

It is the easiest part of the day – the ending of it,
here, with you, among sheets that smell of our skin.
I would know your skin in the dark: its smooth magnetic film
would bring me home and cease my being separate
with one blind touch. I know it again now, this expanse
of noise and light between us. It conquers distance.

Hallways of childhood friends had smells, family smells
that followed family members into school as stowaways
in coat sleeves and lunchboxes – slipped giveaways
of origin, of who made who, of what was left to tell
made suddenly clear in every detail as if recently rained on.
One was made of wine; one walked crushed by blankets even under sun;

one carried the antiseptic of insulin packets and coconut dust
about her, in her hair, and later what I knew by force
to be the thin, hard odour of divorce –
shipyard metal caving under sparks, spit, boot polish and rust.
And I knew also that whatever was in my hallway
was exposing the line and the set of my spine like an x-ray.

Now we too have an identity –
the smell of us is through our sheets and wrapped around our home –
invisible ink encoded onto bone.
We have wrought it as surely as any family
forges something wholly themselves and wholly different
and marks each child for life with the hidden nature of their generative act.

From you, the smell of the Tucson desert:
copper deposits, animal skulls, the chalk trajectory
of stars no cloud covers or stains, ochre and chilli.
From me, bog cotton, coal fires, wild garlic, river dirt.
And from the two of us, salt. When we move house
such genealogies as these will follow us.

LUCIDITY

I

Every night he meets his family, is crumpled with his sisters
in a cellar, or watches as his niece becomes
smaller and smaller until she disappears.

He hides boxes from his mother
that hold the bones of elephants, a warrant for arrest,
the shirts of her own buried father.

Caught either in scenarios of rescue, or with some
bear trap which he's used to trap and kill a man
in Mexico, he knows the man's his brother.

II

Awake, he never phones or writes
and seems so far away in life and mind
from where they are. Amnesia would be kinder –

instead he wants to be a lucid dreamer, to enter
whatever sea of fear and fever
awaits him when he falls. He wants to change the colour

of what's been seen and said, way back,
in the place
he can't remember or forget.

III

Suddenly he wanders, attaching
notes to walls: *am I dreaming? If I meet
my family, then I'm dreaming…*

They cover the house and the whites of his daylight eyes.
Still, every night his family rises
and the smell of harm, the taste of damage

invades him like the rush of a narcotic. He never knows he could escape it
with the thought: *this is a dream, and everything that happens
is a trick…* until he wakes.

IV

*There is an open sky. The kind you find
in desert in November. White clouds go over
at terrible speed. The sky*

*is changing always. There are no ridges
on the land, no corners. At the end
of everything, waving on the ledge*

*of the world, pilots are stumbling to find
their plane. And I am moving backwards, into the source of wind
while they grow*

smaller and smaller until they disappear.

ON WAITAKERE DAM
for Charles Brown

You wanted to up-end the boat
and set it on the lake we lived by
because no one would know.
It was lavish with silverfish and looked
defeated, humped on its secret
like a hand. There was nowhere to go to

but the magnet of the middle lake
where a vapour sat wide as Australia –
as sovereign, as separate, as intimate
with daylight, as ignorant
of clocks and raincoats and boats.
It threw a soft, unwatchable shimmer

we would not be human in.
You dismantled a sky
as you tipped the boat over,
the nest of a possum was robbed.
The hull settled outside-in
as you inverted the universe.

We bobbed in the reeds.
The trees lay down their crowns
beneath us, an underwater canvas
of spectacular women. Above us
the crowds of their branches were cold.
Black swans were nesting in the nesting place,

trees reared to the rim of vision –
we slid on to the centre. At night,
with no lights for miles, the lake
would glitter with the Southern Cross.
It smiled at us
with a million silver teeth.

We'd heard it roar with rain
and watched it coughing eels
over the dam's brim,
too water-sore to keep them any longer.
They fell flinching themselves
into s's or n's.

And now we sat stilled in a boat
in the centre, under the lake's shroud,
and the listening
was for the car of the caretaker –
weaving down from the Nihotipu Dam
with Handel or Bach on the radio.

GOLDFISH

The black fish under the bridge was so long I mistook it
for a goldfish in a Japanese garden the kind the philosophers
wanted about them so much gold underwater to tell them what waited
in another element like breathing water they wanted to go
to the place where closing eyes is to see

I understood the day I closed my eyes in Gifu City I saw Japan
for the first time saw what I had seen the gate to the Nangu
Shrine by the Shinkansen stood straddled before my head and I
held out my hands to touch it and felt changed air it wasn't
there but I walked into it continually and over the gardens full
of pumpkin seeds in the ground and wild red flowers over them they
                                                        told me

they brought autumn and they were about my head also in Gifu City all
                                                        pearled
in mist and happy as Japanese brides. I saw the JR crates on the night
trains that passed through stations and seemed endless and running
on purpose on time's heels on sheer will to cross Honshu one end
to the other money's own messenger fire down the line. And when you
                                                talked me through

Gifu one end to the other eyes closed I saw what I would never
have seen sighted a transvestite taxi driver set apart on the street
a lost person flowers by the pavement pavements for the blind I saw
music as pulled elastic bands drums as the footprints of exacting gods

I mistook the black fish for an oriental goldfish the flash of gold
on its belly meant it carried its message for the element below it
always one storey down Zen masters attaining one storey down and I,
falling into you, story by story, coming to rest in the place where closing
eyes is to see

SPRING FESTIVAL

My body has become the body of the festival:
the vaginas on shrines reduce me to the facts of life.
And my wedding vows to you are this festival's promises –

a roaring in the ears, narrow entrances,
and the two of us hauled into life's own procession
of mother after mother after mother.

SUMMER FESTIVAL

What do you think when you see a mâché vagina
being rammed with a penis as broad as a battering ram
so that children disguised as elements shriek with joy?

You think: *we are disembodied, while the moon herself has a body.*
She is over by the beer stands disguised as a man. One stagger and she'll trigger
the collapse of the dancers. The moon came to watch us and we all fell down.

AUTUMN FESTIVAL

The fields have been sealed with fire. They are singing
the promise of resurrection and revenge. The whole *cho*
 scraped of rice and fruit, it is time to go under and store.

In the streets I watch women who are dancing in rings
in the slow, hindered steps of the kimono. Again and again,
a festival of women. They are declaring what's been done.

WINTER FESTIVAL

They'll padlock themselves with sake against the cold.
They'll bandage their loins. They'll straddle a drum on its side
made from pulled skin and the sign of an upright swastika

and they'll move on a sea of bare men's shoulders, tall as trees,
banging only when the silence has become unendurable.
In the alley there's a pyramid of bright flesh and lanterns, refusing to be born.

TO IMAGINE AN ALPHABET

Too far back to imagine
It all was dissolved
Under soft black strokes
Of a Chinese brush
Diminishing the fatness
Of original things

Animal legs and human legs are emptied of flesh and blood

Patterns from flattened
Ants or a lake drained the facts
That are trees in winter
The spokes of the world went down
In a language that
Went everywhere, stayed put

Put out what you want a woman and man to be the picture will hold
that too

There are stories in skeletons
And after the three fluid
Lines that are Mountain, the four
That are Fire, Ice as a stroke
On the left side of Water –
Problem is Tree in a Box

I hear moaning and see constriction in a picture the colour is cinnamon
the taste is chalk

A mind is inside the lines
All of it and sooner or later
Sex is everywhere, money
Rice fields wives are mostly
Under the roof to like
Is Woman with Child

I get lost in a landscape of noisy ideas that cross and flare in fireworks of
strokes

Like a child who paints a smile
Over signatures makes Yin
And Yang (two kissing fish)
A rising sun in a field
Of wheat I draw windows leaking
On the kanji for Rain

I make my moon round my forest has branches my people are walking
with arms and a head

And then murder comes, a second
Killing, so softly I'm deaf
At the second of entrance.
My pictures defy the eyes.
I see Lamentation as five falling stars,
Grief abroad and walking,

And a terrible stag, flames shooting from his heart, as he prepares to
walk and preach.

No one seems sure of the reason why aprons
are tied to the necks of stone babies in temples.
The priest says 'honour'.
The guide to Kyoto City mentions 'cold
on their journey away from us to the heaven for children'.
I look at them squatting in Buddha-reflection,
wrapped up to the throat in teddy bears and trains.

*

There's a graveyard for miscarriages under Ikeda Mountain
as stark as a bone field. No flowers, tangerines, sake or aprons
but a basin of stone bodies in two parts: square body, round head.
Like oriental soldiers contained by a wall, they would go walking –
spill over with all of the energy for life that fell out of them too soon.
Except that even in stone some bodies have opened –
loose balls in the basin where heads have rolled.

*

Inside the biggest wooden building in the world
sits Japan's greatest Buddha. One hand raised as a stop sign to evil.
The other is flat, flat with comfort and promise, flat enough
for all of us to nuzzle his thumb. His lily flower opened.
His crossing was a falling into light.
Fall with me, he says, *and you'll be raised to the heights
of the roof of the biggest wooden building in the world.*

*

When Nagasawa visits the house of the dead
he leaves at the door his camera and tripod
his champion karaoke voice his miracle foot massage
his classroom dynamics his rockhard atheism
and slips onto the tatami of the prayer room
as the man who can chant any you-name-it soul
between here and Ogaki to paradise.

from THE STATE OF THE PRISONS (2005)

FLIGHT

There he saw one Anne Bridlestone drove through the streets by an officer of the same corporation, holding a rope in his hand, the other end fastened to an engine called the branks, which is like a crown, being of iron with a great gag or tongue of iron; and that is the punishment which magistrates do inflict upon chiding and scolding women; and he hath often seen the like done to others.

ENGLAND'S GRIEVANCE DISCOVERED (1655)

After the murder of our blessèd Martyr,
After the slaughter of the rout at Worcester,
His son the rightful King went into hiding –
Here as a woodcutter, there as a serving-man –
Disguising the telltale milk-white of His skin
By the dye of rotted walnuts. 1651:
The Year of Our Lord that my husband bridled me
And I have learned to hold my tongue in company.

*

He could not remain unrecognised for long,
Majesty being so natural unto Him,
It soon shone forth. But was He loved!
He walked upon the bones of England,
Sought solace at farms and hid in the crowns of trees
And all of nature shadowed Him. His enemies
Sifted the land and still His face was not revealed.
It is my love of Him bleeds when I speak out loud.

*

He has stood in a fall of rain
While Cromwell's men sang psalms against Him
And did not venture in. He has seen women
Sink to their knees and then raise their hand in blessing.
My husband desires a sign.
But for all his reading of *Revelation*
I say heaven admits its own
And it is Him. The jaw-straps tighten.

*

The changeling Prince vanished to France.
Deadwinter dismembers us.
Christmas consumes its own bright fire
And blazes by its absence. There is too much law
To live by, and I have torn my face
In two by swallowing silence.
My husband leads me through the marketplace
As the village women gape.

GENETICS

My father's in my fingers, but my mother's in my palms.
I lift them up and look at them with pleasure –
I know my parents made me by my hands.

They may have been repelled to separate lands,
to separate hemispheres, may sleep with other lovers,
but in me they touch where fingers link to palms.

With nothing left of their togetherness but friends
who quarry for their image by a river,
at least I know their marriage by my hands.

I shape a chapel where a steeple stands.
And when I turn it over,
my father's by my fingers, my mother's by my palms

demure before a priest reciting psalms.
My body is their marriage register.
I re-enact their wedding with my hands.

So take me with you, take up the skin's demands
for mirroring in bodies of the future.
I'll bequeath my fingers, if you bequeath your palms.
We know our parents make us by our hands.

PILOTS

It was black as the slick-stunned coast of Kuwait
over Belfast Lough when the whales came up
(bar the eyelights of aeroplanes, angling in into the airport
out of the east, like Venus on a kitestring being reeled
to earth). All night they surfaced and swam
among the detritus of Sellafield and the panic
of godwits and redshanks.

      By morning
we'd counted fifty (species *Globicephala melaena*)
and Radio Ulster was construing a history. They'd left a sister
rotting on a Cornish beach, and then come here, to this dim
smoke-throated cistern, where the emptying tide leaves a scum
of musselshell and the smell of landfill and drains.
To mourn? Or to warn? Day drummed its thumbs
on their globular foreheads.

      Neither due,
nor quarry, nor necessary, nor asked for, nor understood
upon arrival – what did we reckon to dress them in?
Nothing would fit. Not the man in oilskin working in the warehouse
of a whale, from the film of Sir Shackleton's blasted *Endurance*,
as though a hill had opened onto fairytale measures
of blubber and baleen, and this was the money-
god's recompense;

                              not the huge Blue
seen from the sky, its own floating eco-system, furred
at the edges with surf; nor the unbridgeable flick
of its three-storey tail, bidding goodbye to this angular world
before barrelling under. We remembered a kind of singing,
or rather our take on it: some dismal chorus of want and wistfulness
resounding around the planet, alarmed and prophetic,
with all the foresight we lack –

                              though not one of us
heard it from where we stood on the beaches and car-parks
and cycle-tracks skirting the water. What had they come for?
From Carrickfergus to Helen's Bay, birdwatchers with binoculars
held sway while the city sat empty. The whales grew frenzied.
Children sighed when they dived, then clapped as they rose
again, Christ-like and shining, from the sea, though they could have been
dying out there,

                              smack bang
in the middle of the ferries' trajectory, for all we knew.
Or attempting to die. These were Newfoundland whales,
radically adrift from their feeding grounds, but we took them
as a gift: as if our own lost magnificent ship
had re-entered the Lough, transformed and triumphant,
to visit us. As if those runaway fires on the spines of the hills
had been somehow extinguished…

                              For now,
they were here. And there was nothing whatsoever to be said.
New islands in the water between Eden and Holywood.

CONTRAIL

Nightly now, insomnia lays its thumb
upon my forehead – an any how, Ash Wednesday cross.
Which, instead of insisting *Thou Shalt Pass*

to the Angel of Anxiety, hovering over the stairway,
beckons it in, at 3am, to unsettle me gently
with its insidious wings

Sometimes my mother and father.
Sometimes neither.
Sometimes childlessness, stretching out into the ether

like a plane

CHINA

1

Tack up a screen before dawn and ready the inks.
There is a country which does not exist and which must be shown.
Steady the ingredients.

2

A tunnel of trees. My brother and I on the top
of an empty double-decker in Derbyshire.
The absence-from-home of summer
becoming a scab to be picked over. The bus pulled up

by a pub, as the greenery scratching
at the window ended and we were given a field
with a horse and a dog and a red child
in it, waving.

Sunlight was there like a wall
and halved everything. In my head I was singing
This is Happening This is Happening This is Happening.
A boy bounced his way down the aisle

and started smoking, when time
opened. Or stopped. Or almost stalled
and the boy and my brother and the bus and the world
disappeared on the prick of a needle – pop! – and I

sat sideways avoiding the gap.
And then I saw I was enormous
and in another kind of tunnel. That I was lost.
That there was no going back.

3

Conjure the Yangtze and the Yellow River
And bring them a matter of hours together
On the same train line and both of them seen
Through semi-darkness on a flickering screen
Which is and is not a window. Blow
Over the waters to buckle them. Add snow.

4

The King of the Sea
is awash with vainglory
in Beijing.

He has caused havoc
with his aquatic
animals. Now

he wants to clobber
the Monkey King
(the destined-to-win

Monkey King)
who is wagging his tongue
for some rust-free weapons

from the Sea King's
underwater arsenal.
The Sea King's antennae

are aquiver
with put-upon-
power. The Monkey King,

in his ecstatic
clothing, is too yellow
to be trusted.

The Sea King's refusal
amuses him.
He is fluid

as a cartoon and brimful
with trickery.
He does not know

how colour
is protected.
In a square

given over
to the Palace Executioner
the cobblestones

are mimicking the sun.
For coming too close
to the Only One –

See the desiccated yellows
of the colour convicts
flutter and flare.

5

Evening. Beijing. And farewell to Mao's mausoleum
through the glass, ablaze in the nerves of the Square of Heaven
like everlasting Christmas. The bus forces us on:
another station, another train, another city, another season.
Advertising flickers in the waiting room. That night I dive like a child –
borne aloft by the train's engine, or like one born again in its mild
motion, the shunt and click of the carriages over the sidings
the soporific tenderness of a language I do not recognise –
and re-surface at nine, an hour beyond breakfast time.
The mine wheels, factories, fish farms, and allotments
battling for space between slack-blackened tenements
have receded now into the north. Here the sky is unfolding the blue
cloth of itself on a new country, or on a country which never grew
old to begin with. Spinach, pak choi, cabbage greens, lettuce,
geese sunning themselves among shiny brown cowls of the lotus
and an echo-less emptiness, a sense of perspective too wide
and too high for the eye to take in. Two crows collide
in a rice field, then are flung backwards out of their war
as the train pushes on. We loiter like Oliver in the dining car.
Brunch comes as simmering bowls of noodles, under a film
of oil, and we sit watching the landscape unfurl like a newsreel
into history. By noon, foothills are banking to the south.
By two, we're approaching a network of tunnels blasted out
of the Xi'an Qin Mountains. Blackness falls clean as a guillotine
on the children in pairs by the trackside, and then again
on the man and his son who will walk all afternoon into evening
before they are home. We enter Sichuan without rupturing
any visible line of division, though dinner at five is brimming with chillies:
dried and diced and fried with the seeds inside, while the extraordinary
Sichuan pepper balloons into flavour under our tongues. And all along
darkness is gathering itself in. I see a boy and a woman

lit up by the flare of a crop fire, but can no longer believe in them.
Windows have turned into mirrors the length of the train.
Hours pass, and there is only my white face, strained
in its hopelessness, my failure to catch the day in my hands like a fish
and have it always. The train descends from the soil terraces.
Electricity switches the world back on: town after coal-dusted town
streams by in the rain, revealing its backdoor self, its backyard frown,
until all converge in a dayglo glare at the end of the line and we merge
with our destination. We have been dropped to the bottom of somewhere
blurred and industrial, where the yellow of the Yangtze meets the green
of its tributary, the city with a name like the din of a smithy: Chongqing.

6

All night the hammers broke the dark
But then the dark went on
I rose and pulled the curtains back
A semaphore of cranes

Gesticulating deftly
To each other, to the sky
A city in conspiracy
To keep the sun at bay

And in the fog I could not tell
What was falling down
From what was rising up again
Both wore a hanging chain

And both were eye-less, light-less, stalled
Both held their form elsewhere
The past or future part-way entered
Into this wounded sphere

I left the hold of our hotel
To walk along the river
Across from me, a chargrilled hill
Of building like a fever

And junks that could not carry
The weight of what they bore
Dying in a tributary
Inches from the shore

The sky had almost lightened
To midday's faint resolve
When a mother tugging a wayward child
Brushed against my sleeve

And brought me through a quarter
Of rubble-matted streets
Where a woman washing her waist-length hair
Stood wringing it like a sheet

And stopped me at a doorway
And pointed down its throat
I photographed it dumbly
Lost to what it meant

Her urgency diminished
I smiled I had to go
The air was thick between us
With all I could not know

Day gave without a whimper
I found myself re-caged
Staring through the filter
Of money's privilege

7

I find I have made a ghost
of you – I'm sorry – as I
aimed my camera foolishly
at the passing coloratura
of mountains and fields,
and snapped them anyway,
knowing I'd never get them back
the way they were being given,
at that precise instant, and caught them,
yes alright, adequately enough, but somehow
also caught your watchful face
filling the window without
its source. Confucius refuses
to speak about spirits. *Till you know*
about the living, how are you
to know about the dead? he pronounces
to the ever-curious Tzu-lu.
And I wonder, if I can make ghosts
of the living with my dinky, digital
machine, is it possible I can also
make the dead visible? And I set my camera
more deliberately now on the vast, peopleless
expanse, then check its screen
to see if I've got anything
in its wide-eyed little net.
I don't know what I expected –
one or two of the million Yangtze
drowned, perhaps, still draining their ears
by banging the sides of their heads, or looking after
the vanishing tumult of the train
for directions home?

8

Ever been washed
by a crowd? My mother dragging me
to the cold water tap and
jamming my finger under it
the day I brushed it across

the cooker-top to see
if it was on, *to numb it,*
she said, but it wasn't
like that
at all. It was

winter, we were
baking in the kitchen and
I could still smell a scrap
of skin frying in the background when the cold

hit home – prodding
the length of my arm in a surge
of pain, an ironic
remedy of extremes.
And it was oddly

uplifting to be suspended
there with your body peeled
back to the nerve all
over again in a matter
of seconds, so disarmingly

alive. In four train stations within
fourteen days I turned my head
to a conundrum. After a night
and a day and a night of being carried
along in a capsule –

a bed, a quilt, a pillow, a night-
light, a table, tea, a window,
a radio – I'd uncurl onto
the platform, grey and
exhausted, as though I'd walked

the hours that divided us
from our origin. We were alone
the whole time, moving like
automatons from compartment to
dining car, then back

again, with only the fruit-
man to disturb our corridor
with his casual calling. The train's nose
under the station awning would steam
with exertion; we'd be cracking

our wrists, or avoiding
the press, or yawning, and then,
imperceptibly, finally noticing
the river of people disgorged from a mile
of doors and flooding towards

the exit sign. There must have been
thousands of them, our shadow-
travellers, and we'd been marooned
in the midst of them. They'd have sat
upright all day and

all night on benches as hard
as amazonite, pressed five
to a row and room somehow for
rice pots and rucksacks and armfuls
of jackets, flasks,

blankets. Thirty hours
at a stretch and seeming as fresh
as if they'd just stepped out
of a ten-hour sleep
on a cloud –

and with somewhere to get to
fast: time to stare back
at me the way I was staring
at them, an extravagance.
I stayed to one side, watching

them flow like an out-
going tide into the maw of each
city, and saw myself
caught in the pulse of their
striding, my greenish skin hurled

under water and hammering *I am*
here you are real this
is happening it is
redeemable – as though touching
them might be possible.

9

One day, China met China in the marketplace.
'How are you, China?' asked China, 'we haven't talked in so long.'
China answered: 'The things we have to say to one another,
laid end to end, and side to side,
would connect the Great Wall with the Three Gorges Valley
and stretch nine miles up towards the sun.'
'It's true,' replied China. 'We have a lot to catch up on.'

ON OMITTING THE WORD 'JUST' FROM MY VOCABULARY

And here I am in a room I don't recognise, being
angular and contemporary, with its own
unabashed light source and the table clear.

I must be somewhere Scandinavian.
Where weather is decisively one way
or the other, and summer,

or winter, will not brook contradiction.
Even the ornaments (such as they are)
are purposeful: a stone dog stares into the fireplace

as though pitting itself against fire
for the next quarter-century.
(How you cannot say 'just' and 'pregnancy'.)

There is a fissure in store for me here.
There are no wall hangings. Or rugs.
The door is locked against me.

My own audacity in coming here
astounds me. Yet I step purposefully.
I swell uncontrollably.

Beyond in the hallway
the tongue of a bell is banging against its shell.
It sounds like a coffin lid,

or as definitive.
It is marking the hours until I break into two
and lose/gain everything.

CLOCKS

The sadness of their house is hard to defeat. There are at least three clocks per room.
There are two people with nothing to do but to be in each room and be separate.
The person each room was decorated by was seconded to a plot in a cemetery
that is walked to every day, and tended like a bedroom sanctuary. No notice given.
The clocks do all the talking. He visits the grave in the middle of a three-hour loop
and knows the year of completion of every castle in Ireland. His route
is always the same: the round tower via the aqueduct via the cemetery via the
                                                                        ramparts
via the Battle of Antrim during the Rising of the United Irishmen in 1798,
the slaughter of which is more present if he's deep in the morning
of his April wedding breakfast or locked into the moment they fitted the oxygen
                                                                        mask
and she rolled her bruised eyes back. She is unable to find the stop for the bus
                                                                        to Belfast
and stays indoors. The nets turn the daylight white and empty.
She has worn the married life of her sister so tightly
over her own, the noise of the clocks makes her feel almost without skin.
Sometimes she sits in her sister's chair, and feels guilty.
She has *Countdown* for company and a selective memory –
the argument at the funeral with her niece over jewellery and, years ago,
the conspiracy to keep her single, its success. Time settles over each afternoon
like an enormous wing, when the flurry of lunchtime has left them
and the plates have already been set for tea. He reads extensively –
from *Hitler and Stalin, Parallel Lives*, to *Why Ireland Starved* –
but has taken to giving books away recently to anyone who calls.
Winter or summer, evenings end early: they retire to their separate rooms
at least two hours before sleep. It falls like an act of mercy
when the twenty-two clocks chime eight o'clock in almost perfect unison.

ABSENCES ALSO

Take shape,
our lives seep up
like awareness of the dead

take sup. See
with missing children
among the overly sensitive.

THE YELLOW EMPEROR'S CLASSIC
after Gong Sun

The body is China.
Middle Kingdom between here
and hereafter, it is compromised from the start.
Messengers are important.

China has been an imperial system
for centuries, and repeats itself endlessly.
The heart is its Emperor.
All other organs are the Emperor's courtiers –

see poor pericardium
go slack with deflected shame.
A king may never be blamed directly, so
heart-sac swallows heart-blows uncomplainingly.

We are constantly at the mercy
of pernicious influences: cold, damp, dry, wind,
heat and summer heat. (There are two kinds
of summer in the Chinese calendar.)

These are also known as the six evils.
When the spirit exits, it exits
from the back of the neck. The body
opens and shuts itself to damage

like a gate refusing to be latched.
We muster control
of our orifices.
We fight back.

Sexual energy resides in the kidney,
lowest of all yin organs
and root of the body tree.
Desire is pre-heaven essence.

It flows before birth,
bestowed wherever our souls
are stowed, in a limited vial
and fatally expendable.

There is a highway
of sexual awakening,
a road rather than a river
in spite of water.

At puberty a dignitary
(from heaven, ultimately)
slashes with his sword the bloodsilk
ribbon and cries 'Open!'

Old Liver General
must ensure all *qi* troops
now pass
in an orderly fashion.

For there must be sex. True, too much
depletes our pre-heaven essence
and can result in weaknesses
of the lower trunk. But too little is catastrophic.

Like trying to survive
without our opposite
inside us
when opposites equal life.

China is haunted by celibate women
at risk from surfeit of yin. Listen.
Withering from within, they are homesick
and wandering. Vengeful as ghosts.

ZERO
for Joseph

Whatever else it was he stole from the East –
indigo, gold, a brace of abused and temporary women,
frankincense, the inevitable spice or two,
or the fruit that shed itself with such feral sweetness
on the tongue it begged re-naming –
Alexander also stowed nothing –
that double nick in the Babylonian plaque which,
of everything, was the easiest to store
(the women were a nightmare)
precisely because it lived nowhere
and therefore everywhere: in two spare horseshoes
angled together, in the kiss of a thumb and forefinger,
in the sigh at the bottom of a poured-out water jar,
in the memory of some noon-white city square
wherever luck ran out, or faith, or anger –

                                                            but

when Alexander delivered zero to the Greeks
they turned and saw (or thought they saw)
a wellhead blacken in front of them –
an incredulous, bricked-in 'O' –
unravelling into inkiness like a sleeve, the kind
you might toss a stone into and never hear the splash,
though you stand and wait, your ear awash in silence,
for an hour – and over it the bric-a-brac of kitchens appeared
suspended in the sunshine – knives, lemons, sieves, pots, bowls –
a funnel of dailyness, which the wellhead then swallowed
like a child, and, sensing where it could lead,
this number/no-number that would eat the world,
the Greeks turned back to Alexander in the advancing shade
and smiled: for there were still angles, there were still
three old angels skipping over heaven carrying harps and signs.

STEPFATHER

When Cathy came to New Zealand, my stepfather
Charles put on his woollen vest and Swan overcoat and peaked cap
with a rainbow embroidered on it and took us to see the waterfall.

He was a bushman: had grown up in the bush Up North
before ever there was a town the way Whangarei is a town today
with its flat whites and yellow taxicabs and Maori women drivers. Yes,

had shouldered his way into adulthood, into being army-wed,
from the bed of an eel-breeding creek, on the back of a Kauri trunk,
against the hard flat palm of a forest that – decades afterwards –

had still not been felled. So he knew where to take us and how to take us,
that winter afternoon, in the handclapping rain of the Waitakeres,
donning that pack of his as though he were back in Vietnam,

where all his booming dreams still happen, his casual jockey saunter
a bowsprit through the leaves, though he knew exactly what we might find
and wasn't daunted. And yet how tenderly they would park their cars –

some even bothering to hood the steering wheel in chains –
in viewing spots anywhere along the Scenic Drive, before breaking off
into the trees, when he would get the call to go and find them.

He'd cut them down after days sometimes. The branches of Pongas
unfisted beside the railway line and the birds were indefatigable.
The rain was bringing the dark on early but you could still see

the entire steaming basin of greenery swallowing water
on your left side (my mother in her innocence asking,
the day she arrived from Ireland, *but who planted all this?*)

and Cathy and Joseph and Charles and I were increasingly more like
forked poles in a river than people as we came up to the mouth
of the train tunnel and waded inside. He could woo wood pigeons

just by talking to them and once one had rested on his hand.
Away from the thwack and clatter of the downpour and where
entrance and exit were two equidistant reminders of daylight

lived the glow-worms he spoke of, that were not worms at all
but a little boy's peel-and-stick galaxy, a lace of green needlepoint,
winking on after lights-out over the bunk bed. Out at the other end

and evening was gathering pace in the forest far faster than we'd predicted,
returning each towering layer of flax to one vast, dripping canopy.
By the rudiments of a siding shed – a rejected Korean asylum seeker

had survived here for a fortnight on trapped possums and stream water –
we angled ourselves for the climb and veered right, up through the breathing
trees, and what dusk there was had swung shut on a solitariness

of moss and lichen and spider orchids. Charles cut the way out in front of us
without slowing, insisting we still had time, his mind – who knows –
on the nights he'd lain down on the floor of a Singapore jungle,

with only a net to shelter in, and the insects in the air had shrieked
so accusingly at every rigid angle of his body, he couldn't sleep.
It had been raining now for a week. The Waitakere Dam was full –

even from here we could hear it batter itself over the brim
and the waterfall was the same: choked and slick and incandescent
in the dim cave it had made for itself. Our breaths came hard

and alien in the clearing as we took its kiss on our skin.
Charles stood like a conquistador, hand on one hip, looking up.
But already I was imagining the journey back, down through the slithering

dark, all three of us steady in his flashlight's wake, hitting the railway track
and then on through the tunnel and then up to the steps by the concrete expanse
of the dam face, and into the house near the watercress bank where my life

had been riveted for months. Our homecoming chorus the hunger
of owls, fierce and unassuageable – *morpork! morpork!* –
and Charles cocking his head at the sound of them as though they could speak.

from THROUGH THE SQUARE WINDOW (2009)

STORM

It was already Gothic
enough, what with that
King-of-Versailles-sized bed
with room for me and two
or three liveried footmen;

wall-lights like candle-shafts
in fake pearl and cut
glass; and the stranded
little girl in the photographs
growing sorrowful –

her cascade sleeves, her floral
crown – as though taken
by Lewis Carroll. All afternoon
the church bells rang out
their warning. Cumulostratus

ascended into heaven.
Evening and the white forked
parting of the sky fell
directly overhead, casements
rattled on hinges and Thunder

may as well have summoned
the raggle-taggle denizens
of his vociferous world:
the ghouls, the gashed, the dead
so bored by now of being

dead they flock to gawk –
sanctuary was still sanctuary
except more so, with the inside
holding flickeringly, and the
outside clamouring in.

SAINT-EXUPÉRY

That the world might be burnt clean by gasoline
exploding in an engine, was completely unforeseen
by Saint-Exupéry, who, after his aeroplane crashed
in the Sahara, saw his former self evaporate like mist –

leaving a thirst like acid on the tongue,
snakes, sun, rocks, and the hypnagogic vision
of a tyrannous, golden prince, whom he rendered later
with blackened eyes like thumbprints off a newspaper.

A DEVICE FOR MONITORING BRAIN ACTIVITY
BY SHINING LIGHT INTO THE PUPIL
after Petr Borkovec

A liner in the foreground of the Lough
– dead-centre but already passing on –
white as a tent in Plantagenet France. I walked
the steep road to the shore, which tips
the earth into ocean,
levers ocean up to heaven,
as though broken in the middle by a hand.
I watched for gulls where the Threemilewater
empties and spills. The liner shone.

Ducks were tugging each other out to sea.
They rode each wave the liner sent
percussively. They wobbled and re-gathered
in the succeeding calm. Across the Lough
– if only for a moment – hillsides
snided in gorse bushes crackled and sang.
A straggle of crows, backs to the enemy,
were guarding the bars fencing the cenotaph
while cormorants out on the platform –

huddled and avuncular and jet-dark
as obsidian – were as standing stones
to the wash beneath them: the tide
advanced, the water glistening.

Smashed mussel shells banked
against the sides of rocks burned blue
in the sun. And though the waves from the ship
still repeated along the bulwark, decreasing
in intensity, the door to the sea floor stood open
in between: sand, weeds, a trolley
taking several hundred years to disappear.
Light fell unequally at the horizon's vanishing-
point as though the edge of the world glared upwards.

The liner shone all the while.
Absorbing the sunlight, throwing it out again.
That shimmering, regal tent, I thought,
is almost like a ship: complete with passengers
and a captain's banquet. It could be that.
Brightness blurred the skin of everything.
I watched the gulls flare white
above the river mouth and saw, in hours,
how their wings, to a still-blue sky, would answer black.

MATTER
for S.P.

Aristotle observed and recorded it all –
that out of rainwater, the marrow
of the human spine, foam from the sea,
or the putrefying carcasses of bulls and horses
spring living beings: frogs, serpents, anchovies,
bees and scarabs, locusts, weevils, maggots.
St Augustine agreed: what matter that the smallest
(and most meddlesome) of God's creatures
find no mention in the chronicle of the Ark?
So long as alluvial mud remained, or rotted
wood, or rinsed white bones of crocodiles
after the wash abated and the salvaged couple
and their braying entourage were pitched
on top of Ararat, wasps and gnats and fleas
would manifest once more in clouds and colonies
without a union of the sexes (like Mary)
and the earth would effortlessly teem.
Recipes for rats and 'small white puppies
a child might play with' followed
during the Middle Ages, which typically included
hay, excrement, dirty shirts, wool
simmered for an hour then hung to dry
in an outhouse or chicken coop
(the air of such places being itself
so mutable and laden with infusoria,
it acts as a bridge to life). Golems
moulded from clay still needed a spell
to keep them animated, as though by
growing bigger and more complicated,
the offspring of the elements
was in danger of winding down,

yet Paracelsus, arch-advocate of decay,
saw no reason not to apply
the laws of spontaneous generation
to ourselves: *let the semen of a man*
putrefy by itself for forty days in a sealed
cucurbite, it shall begin, at last, to live.
Fed on an arcanum of human blood
and kept in darkness, his fleet homunculus
had all the features of a human child.
Leeuwenhoek bore this experiment in mind
when, decades later, using his own microscope,
he scrutinised his sperm, magnified
as much as three hundred times and fashioned
like a bell, with the wrought perfection
of a tiny man curled inside each globule.
Ovists may have envisaged instead
a sacred cabinet of children, encased
inside each egg, opening in time
both backwards and forwards
to the breaking of Eve and the End
of the World, the likelihood remained:
whether one believed in this, or the evidence
of a light-blanched workshop and a knack
for polished glass, or whether one went back
to what the Greeks expressed
as the facts of reproduction,
a woman's quest for contraception,
stacked against the odds of dogged visitors
finding lodging in the womb
at any beckoning, was hopeless.
No wonder Soranus suggested water from blacksmiths'.
No wonder olive oil, the pulp of a pomegranate,
honey, pine resin, mercury, beeswax,
pennyroyal, tobacco juice, arrowroot, tansy

were burnt, brewed, inhaled, ingested,
inserted into the cervix, or buried in fields left fallow
if the coppery stain of menstruation
persisted into the seventh day.
No wonder witches consulted the sky.
And though I know, thanks in part to Pasteur –
to his gauze impediments and penchant
for boiling – how you came to enter,
how you came to roll and hiccup and kick
against the windowless dark, feet to my heart
and skull to the pelvic cradle, I still think
of our lovemaking as a kind of door
to wherever you were, waiting in matter,
spooled into a form I have not yet been shown
by the unprompted action of nature,
by something corrupting in an earthenware pot
in Corinth, say, or Kingstown.
Stay the wind on a river eight weeks after equinox –
witness blue-green mayflies lift off
like a shaken blanket; add algae
and alchemical stones to the lake floor
in the strengthening teeth of winter, what swans.

FOUND ARCHITECTURE
for Kerry Hardie

These days are all about waiting. What would you say
if I tried to explain how my single true activity
this wet and shivery May was 'found architecture'?

As the giver of an Italian kaleidoscope
that makes its heel-toe shapes, not from beads or seeds
or painted meticulous details, but from the room,

from whatever room I happen to be in,
or from the street, always eager and unerringly
democratic, you stand slightly to the south of me

with your head raised and I imagine you smiling.
The day it arrived I mangled the blue of the bathroom
with the pistachio green of my bedroom ceiling

and sat entranced: such symmetrical splicing
of everything, anything, to make of my waiting-house
a star-pointed frame that entered and left

itself behind as the cylinder turned. Any light that there was
was instantly mystical – a crack in the pattern's
typography, like the door at the end of the corridor

shedding radiance. Yesterday evening, by the sea,
a strangled sealed-off swamp by a walkway
threw up, suddenly, the Aboriginal outback:

rotted glands of a pond between knee-high grasses
and a white tree undoing itself in its ink-stained
surfaces. The tree looked like a crocodile's ribcage

as I passed along the perimeter, or the wide-propped
jawbone of a whale. Until it became, the further
I walked, a canoe, asleep on the water and fettered

with algae. Another dead branch sat up
in the grass like the head of an otter and talked.
This, too, was found architecture. And all the usual,

of course: skeletons of geranium leaves on windowsills
long afterwards; snakeskins, clouds.
Beaches are full of it: found architecture being

the very business of beaches. Most recently
(and most disarmingly) this: handed to me in a roll
of four like mug-shot photographs from a machine –

his seahorse spine, his open-shut anemone
of a heart, and the row of unbelievable teeth
shining high in the crook of his skull as though backstitched

into place. From blood and the body's
inconsolable hunger I have been my own kaleidoscope –
five winter-bleached girls on a diving board, ready to jump.

Dearest William –

I could begin by hoping you are well in England
(and I do!) now that the ——th regiment has returned
to Chatham; or I could begin by telling you
that reports of worsening weather here are true;
that Georgie thinks you wicked and unkind
for leaving him; that your former servants pine;
or that father, though no better, is no worse, etc.
But this is not a weather-talk sort of letter.
It is after three. The whole house sleeps
(even Becky) and I am kept awake six weeks
by your crippling absence: an irony, I confess,
since for all your years of passionate presence
I failed to cherish you... Now that you're gone,
Becky (and you were right about her all along)
keeps dreadful company: boorish men who jest
and drink and flirt and she isn't in the slightest
shocked by any of it. I keep to my room.
I have placed the portrait of George face down
on the dresser. I have folded the gloves you left
in an innermost drawer, as though they were a gift.
Since you spoke of my *incapacity* for love
I have come to see how my own fierce widowhood
was a shell against the world, a kind of carapace
made up of pride, stupidity and cowardice,
a stay, if you will, against 'the kind of attachment'
such as yours for me deserved. Poor shredded raiment –
for if it did not keep me warm, it kept me safe,
safe against you and safe against myself.
Last year, at the opera (it was *Dido and Aeneas*),

I wished to take your hand – in a sudden, artless,
harmless way that would not give you pause –
then didn't. I think I must have sensed the charge
built up from a decade's loving in your fingers
(though there you sat, as solid as an anchor)
and feared that touching it would knock me flat.
Now I'm scared I shall die without it.
Dear Dobbin, come back. Like everything else we do
in our mingled, muddy lives, this letter is overdue.
Forgive me if my love arrives belatedly,
but there is a ship can get you here by Friday
and, come all the rain in Christendom,
I shall be waiting for you by the viewing platform.
Dearest William, put out to sea.

Yours, Amelia Sedley.

ICE

They've come & gone before.
        Two hours or so
of a fine rain freezing on impact
        & what passes
for the world in West Quebec
        (woods, sugar-
bush, pylons, sheep) has spangled
        itself in ice.
Branches bend & snap & forests
        for years afterwards
hold their grieving centres bare
        where Pin Oak,
Siberian Elm, Common Hackberry
        & Bradford Pear
perform a shorn prostration & are
        unable to right
themselves; they teach the weeping
        willow how it's
done. Sometimes Frost's broken
        dome of heaven
is how storms end, just that, a shattering
        in the sunlight
of the million crystal filaments
        that fell & hung
on everything, as though absence of
        breath had caused
the general lock-in & simple breath
        was all we ever
needed to un-sleeve the present
        & make it real again.

*

Monday, January 5th: we wake
     to a bluish light
lasering through the window, a wiped
     display on the radio
& the racket of gunshot. The house
     is cold & all
around the trees are coming down.
     First the crack
at the stem of the weight-sore trunk,
     then a clinking
magnified, a china shop upending
     in an earthquake,
as the branches rattle & snag.
     When the whole
tree hits, a volley of shots goes up
     & its burden of glass
explodes. This ten, twenty, fifty times
     until we lose each crash
to the cacophony of the week-long storm.
     I still remember
you standing in your housecoat
     that first night
& how your face was lit by the
     transformer
shorting out outside. We didn't know
     the blackout
ended five states wide, or that the
     footprint
of the ice-storm could be seen
     from space.

*

The sheep were dead. The summary
        execution
of every maple within earshot
        finally stopped
at dawn on the penultimate day.
        The house still
stood, astonished, the one upright
        among a litter
of horizontals, & while it rained
        & froze, rained
& froze, a quiet inside the rainfall
        began to
spread itself abroad, all targets down,
        all debris blown
asunder. You begged me to check
        the sheep.
I knew before I reached them two
        hours later –
the outline of my person hanging
        frozen in the air –
that none of them had survived.
        The silence
was ubiquitous & pure as star-silence.
        So all I had
to offer as I slipped & slithered home-
        wards was an out-
building of kneeling, petrified sheep,
        locked to their
spots like pieces in a Snow Queen's
        game of chess.

                    *

Frost flowers. Bearded trees. Ghosts
        of some sudden
deleterious fungus ballooning out
        of the brushwood
one spectacular rose-bowl morning
        the previous
fall. The lavish, sexual freeze
        of long-stemmed
plants whose ensuing ersatz petals
        splinter when
touched. Midnight, January 9th:
        the jettisoned
excess of the Mississippi Delta
        had punished
us enough. Rain reverted to gas. Before
        the burials, before
the muddy thaw, before the gathering
        mass of melted ice
flooded the south, before the army
        & the extraction
of what was felled from what was
        left, we stood
at our living-room window & watched
        a tiny moon
& a tatter of stars high up in the
        atmosphere
& kissed as two will kiss through sheets
        dipped in dis-
infectant, & everything between us
        flew apart.

'LOVE, THE NIGHTWATCH...'

Love, the nightwatch, gloved and gowned, attended.
Your father held my hand. His hands grew bruised
and for days afterwards wore a green and purple coverlet

when he held you to the light, held your delicate, dented
head, thumbed-in like a water font. They used
stopwatches, clip charts, the distant hoof beats of a heart

(divined, it seemed, by radio, so your call fell intertwined
with taxicabs, police reports, the weather blowing showery
from the north) and a beautiful fine white cane,

carved into a fish hook. I was a haystack the children climbed
and ruined, collapsing almost imperceptibly
at first, then caving in spectacularly as you stuttered and came

– crook-shouldered, blue, believable, beyond me –
in a thunder of blood, in a flood-plain of intimate stains.

AUGUSTINE SLEEPING BEFORE HE CAN TALK

The only places he can dive to are the senses.
The Christmas lights his father dangled from the corners
of his ceiling in July are his palimpsest for the world –
a winking on and off of ebullient colour, unnamed and so untamed,
to be committed to memory and then written over.
For now the world is simply to be crawled into, like the sea,
of which he has no fear, a bubbling, transmogrifying, all-
attracting mechanism that has not yet disappointed
with the mean-spirited vanishing act of an ink-black horizon.
He has already learned how the tongue contains more mystery
than the granite hulk of an elephant swaying suddenly into focus
under the dank and knotted overhang of Cave Hill, tossing
straw onto its shoulders to keep itself warm because it still
– and tragically – remembers Africa, that when he opens
his mouth to admit the spoon, anything can happen,
from passion fruit to parmesan. The three tributary-
sounds of his name that flow as one (as though summer's
hottest month had a feminine ending) he knows, and the purring
of cats and cars and the howling of dogs and fireworks.
His fingers adjust the tufts of the sheepswool coat
he lies on in his sleep. Tomorrow I'll offer him the dent
of a worry stone and the fluted sticky centres of acacia flowers.
All this can only be where he goes – there can be no other possibility –
unless we accept that memory begins in the womb or back,
still further, in the undiscovered bourne poor Hamlet dreamed
of entering without map or compass as a deliverance
from the sight of our back garden in September, the apple tree
keeled over and cankered and the fuchsia disrobed.
If he ever bombs inside a swimming-pool, or deep-sea dives,
or moon-walks, if he ever moves from balancing

on some underwater floor, precariously filled with air,
to pressing off on the balls of his feet into his own ascent,
through a dense and illegible element, he may remember
what it felt like to wake when he was one, and that it was
a slow, alert surfacing towards the morning, the clock's face,
the seagulls and the sea's address, all clamouring to be experienced.

THROUGH THE SQUARE WINDOW

In my dream the dead have arrived
to wash the windows of my house.
There are no blinds to shut them out with.

The clouds above the Lough are stacked
like the clouds are stacked above Delft.
They have the glutted look of clouds over water.

The heads of the dead are huge. I wonder
if it's my son they're after, his
effortless breath, his ribbon of years –

but he sleeps on unregarded in his cot,
inured, it would seem, quite naturally
to the sluicing and battering and paring back of glass

that delivers this shining exterior…
One blue boy holds a rag in his teeth
between panes like a conjuror.

And then, as suddenly as they came, they go.
And there is a horizon
from which only the clouds stare in,

the massed canopies of Hazelbank,
the severed tip of the Strangford Peninsula,
and a density in the room I find it difficult to breathe in

until I wake, flat on my back with a cork
in my mouth, bottle-stoppered, in fact,
like a herbalist's cure for dropsy.

THE CLANGERS
for Gerald Boyle

This planet, this cloudy planet, is the Earth.
We cannot guess how flawed and insignificant it is
unless we travel, in our imaginations, to another star –
to another stone-pocked sphere without atmosphere
where an orderly people, curious and conciliatory,
stares out across the vast and silent territory
of intergalactic space, dreaming of otherness…

…which arrived, once,
in the shape of an iron chicken
they cobbled together from sky detritus.
It couldn't understand its own coordinates
and blundered all over the meteor garden
until Tiny Clanger – *there now there* –
calmed it into submission like a horse whisperer.
As thanks it laid an iron egg before flapping away
to its spiky nest. The egg was filled with staves
which Tiny Clanger planted and watched turn into music trees.

On other star-bright days, when otherness
fails to visit them, the Clangers resort to flying machines
to snatch whatever passing implement or instrument they can.
Flying machines are Major Clanger's passion.
It is the randomness of sky-fishing that excites him:
a functioning television set or a hat with live inhabitants –
whatever the harvest is, it must be clamorously exhibited
for the benefit of everyone, then taken
on a trolley to the Soup Dragon.

Inside the Clanger planet
there are caves and caves and caves full of flowers
and only the glow-buzzers know they are there at all.
Small Clanger got lost once, like all the countless dead before

                                          Theseus,

following the glow-buzzers to the glow-honey source.
At first he didn't notice: the caves an enticement of pearly lights
and unexpected airiness, the flowers a theatre.
While Granny Clanger nodded over her knitting
he was bowing to each extraordinary face in turn.
(Eventually, the glow-buzzers led him out again.)

Goodbye Clangers! That stretched and iridescent shawl
of stars and dark between your world and ours is beckoning…
Tuck yourselves into bed. Fold your ears over your eyes.
Whistle your singing-kettle breath one last time.

The Plasterers: *The Creation*
The Cardmakers: *The Creation of Adam and Eve*

    The Fullers: *Adam and Eve in Eden*
    The Armourers: *The Expulsion*

The Shipwrights: *The Building of the Ark*
The Fishers and Mariners: *The Flood*

    The Parchmentmakers and Bookbinders: *Abraham and Isaac*
    The Pewterers and Founders: *Joseph's Trouble about Mary*

The Tilethatchers: *The Nativity*
St Leonard's Hospital: *The Purification*

    The Vintners: *The Marriage at Cana*
    The Cappers: *The Woman Taken in Adultery*

The Bakers: *The Last Supper*
The Cordwainers: *The Agony in the Garden and the Betrayal*

    The Bowers and Fletchers: *Christ Before Annas and Caiaphas*
    The Tapiters and Couchers: *The Dream of Pilate's Wife*

The Butchers: *The Death of Christ*
The Cooks and Waterleaders: *The Remorse of Judas*

    The Tailors: *The Ascension*
    The Potters: *Pentecost*

And episodes in between with a yet more fabulous cohabiting:
The Woolpackers and Woollenweavers: *The Assumption of the Virgin*

The Spurriers and Lorimers: *Christ and the Doctors*
The Spicers: *The Annunciation*, and

Because even a singing gash in the stratosphere is redeemable,
The Fall of Man
To the repairers of barrels, buckets, and tubs.

Dear Heart, I dreamed a territory so seeming rich
and decorous, I woke with all its workings on my tongue.
Napoleon vanquished Europe. But when he died
(of natural causes) on the Palace-Garden Isle, Isola Bella,
built to resemble the rigging of ships, the map changed colour
from the Bay of Biscay to the Carpathian Peaks as bloodlessly
as the delicate octopus its rippling skin. The world shrugged off
his atheistic scarlet and dipped itself in yellow, the yellow of egg-
yolk and daylight's origin, and a Golden Age let down its iron bridge
and set us travelling. Everywhere was the same: commerce
was encouraged (though not excessively); order and cleanliness
governed and dignified both public and private realms; music
and poetry could be heard in all quarters. In Spain itself, the centre
of the Empire, all were as one: Language, Religion, the Crafts of State,
and the people flourished and were happy, the sap in the veins
of a Body Politick in rigorous health. Women, ever the lynchpin,
of households and families, of the men who bear the imperial
                                                            message
like a lamp into the dark, wore their mantle lightly, were softly
spoken, modestly attired, and though at liberty to work and roam
abroad, turned all their passion inwards to their sons and homes...

Dear Heart,

travelling through Switzerland in a previous summer, we stopped
in Berne and witnessed the *Zytglogge*: a medieval tower of time.
Beneath its east main face is an intricate astronomical and astrological
device, wherein, in one small radius, are displayed:
all twenty-four hours, the hours of brightness, the days
of the week, our position in the zodiac, the date, the month, the progress
of the moon and the degree of elevation of the sun on the horizon.

It was raining that straightforward, European rain we seldom see
at home and a small crowd murmured to their umbrellas
as Caspar Brunner's parade of bears, Chronos with his hourglass,
and a grinning jester in cap and bells rattled out of the darkness
four minutes to the hour. And my dream was like this –
as these eight signposts to our mortal existences
clicked and chimed together, so the interlocking arms
of God and Man and Government danced flawlessly there.
What measure of exactness could keep my golden territory
intact and accurate to the second? That same year, but later,
a woman read my fortune in a brace of cards. One showed a cup,
for love, and another a blinded girl, and another a hill of wheels
and gibbets, stood stark against the sky as the Saviour's Cross.

FLU

When flu arrived that winter, I was ill for weeks.
Even my eyes were infected. I lay back and hallucinated –
the light was a flesh balloon; his face, when he came
with bitter effervescence, a bitten-through moon

or thigh bone...   After that, I slept
or stared at *A Century of Russian Photographs.*
Anastasia's chocolate frown. Lenin on his stack.
Lily Brik with her horseshoe teeth and headscarf.

And then page after page of unreadable scenes
I couldn't get the measure of, like the clusters of dots
in a magazine, containing a fortress
or Tyrannosaurus rex if you only knew how to lose focus.

The afternoons were quietest.
The streets outside my window held snow and letterboxes.

FAIRGROUND MUSIC

The fair had come. It must have been Whitsun.
They'd camp every year at the end of our yard –
you could hear the screams and the grinding of the rides
and a noise like whizz-bangs from the house.
Tom had taken Hazel off to get lost in it
so I had the kitchen to myself. Which was larger,
somehow, and scented, and lonely. I was baking scones.

It was Esther gave me the shock – *hello Doris* –
standing in the door-frame like a ghost.
She'd been riding all afternoon: the dipper,
the dodgems, the giant wheel. You could tell
she was five months gone just by looking at her.
She needed the privy – *it would save me the walk* –
and I said alright because she was family.

She was out there an age. I had the scones in the oven
and the table scrubbed and the dishes washed
and draining on the rack and was wondering
if she'd stumbled on the garden path
when she came back, grey as a newspaper.
She put a hand to her hair and straightened her frock.
See you at church, then. Give Tom my best –

And then she left. I waited till the scones were finished,
dried my hands on a tea-towel, slipped my rings
from the windowsill, and made my way
past the rain barrel and the rabbit hutch to the door
of the outhouse, which was shut. Spiders' webs,
threaded like a lattice, covered the blistering paint.
I lifted the latch.

Inside, blood was everywhere: on the floor, on the walls.
You could tell where Esther had walked
by a set of white shadows. And then I saw her child –
bigger than the span of my hand and furred,
its fingers were curled near its ears and its eyelids were veined.
Its back was to the bowl. It was a girl.
I couldn't take my eyes off it, until I remembered

where I was and what had happened,
and stepped out onto the path and went back to the kitchen.
The sounds from the fair seemed louder
after that: hurdy-gurdy music and the cries of the ticket sellers
ratcheting up for the evening…
I sat at the table, waiting for Tom to come in.
The ceiling caught the colours of the machines.

CATHEDRAL

As though the world were a spiral staircase,
and the order in which you ascended it
already set, I wanted the words
you attempted first to be solid and obvious:
apple, finger, spoon. The bat
hanging like a blister in your drool-proof
baby book or the lovesick cricket
with its gossamer instrument
were surely to be held back:
until I could explain, until I could build
you a zoo of improbable candidates
and properly introduce you.
But you were too quick –
like panic, there was no stopping it –
each day's vast, unbreachable
impact – and language,
in whatever ramshackle order
it made its presence felt –
a movable moon, the guts
of a clock, a fire escape –
rained down and into you, like
Catherine Linton's wine-through-water
dream of the heath and expulsion
from heaven. I cannot hang
a curtain to keep it off. I cannot
section it. It is entering via
the ear's aqueduct, every
listening second, trickling in
to its base equilibrium
and carrying with it an image in negative
to be absorbed by the brain and stored.

Bah! humbug! you say, aged two,
like the terrible man
in the cape with the walking stick
you glimpsed in the afternoon,
and what we assumed you knew
is jolted on its axis; then this:
at six o'clock the ghost
of a child might come and eat porridge.
We are speechless.

Her father was born in Arkansas, the youngest, loneliest child
in a family of five. They lived in a four-roomed house
in a middle-sized town. When America went to war, he witnessed
columns of volunteers, filing out beyond the window,
singing, how fires on the street corners opposite blunted the night.
When his brothers got shot, he knew it was all his fault.

His mother was meticulous in punishment. So many faults
accrued to him, like interest, turning a fair-haired, freckled child
into a cross, she grew ingenious. If he wet the bed at night
(which he often did) she'd parade him through the house,
wrapped in a steaming sheet, to the frame of a backlit window,
so that people passing below might notice and be witness

to such wickedness. Other punishments went unwitnessed:
the confiscated meals, the bleeding feet. He was faulted
for speaking, and for keeping quiet. Mooning by the window
when his mother wasn't looking, he imagined himself a different child
in a different kind of country, Mexico perhaps, or Texas, in a house
that, barring moonlight, would be kept completely dark at night –

no standing lamps to shame him by… One night
while his parents slept, he ran away. There were no witnesses.
He left no note. He extracted himself from the house
like oil devolving itself from water, and found a job repairing faults
for the national telegraph company. Though still technically a child
(at seventeen) he knew this was his window

to the life he'd always dreamed of, a window
that would shut and lock before his twenty-first year. On a

                                      star-shot night
in Boulder, Colorado, he was married to Anne, who cried like a child,
while her father glowered beside them, their only witness.
The sex was her fault for being curious, the foetus her fault
that made her sick and saw them stuck in a four-roomed house

in a middle-sized town, so like the house
back home in Arkansas, his spirit failed him. Two small windows
stared onto the street. Anne grew silent, obedient to a fault.
Six months after the wedding, at ten past midnight,
Anne clutching the iron bedpost, the doctor arrived to witness
the birth of Mary Ruby Evans, their first and final child.

Whose fault that for twelve years afterwards in that house
a man slipped into the room of a child, kept back from the tiny

                                            window,
and nightly undid what only the hawk moths witnessed?

THE HANGING HARE

Once, a boy
with a bare brown chest
brought a hare to our back door.
It was heavy summer: the alleyway
he walked along held August's
bin-lid stink & stupor.
He wouldn't stay,

declared the hare
a present from his father.
My brother fetched a length of string,
tied it by its feet, then watched as our mother
fastened it carefully to the iron banister
where it spun like the spiraling
seed of a sycamore,

losing momentum...
Soon enough it hung there
motionless, impaled upon its own
frozen direct line of perfect martyrdom,
its eye an abyss, its foxglove fur
unblemished bar the torn
& matted abdomen

where the shot
went in. I could have sat
at the foot of the flight of stairs
for hours to get the measure of it (its ear-tips
dipped in black against the almost-white
of its ears' interiors!) if my mother
had allowed it.

She banished me
outside, where the afternoon
lay festering, & yet it almost seemed as if
the sunken playground, hacked-out stumps of trees
& blackened mattresses where a fire had been
were wiped out by this gift,
this legacy

of unimpeded air,
of whitethorn-quartered fields
for miles around, of granular traces
still on the skin from a swimmable river,
of plovers' eggs, the calyx-wheels
of larkspur, of spaces
where a hare

might flourish...
Like a sideshow hawker
with a star exhibit, I rounded in
the street, before my father skinned & washed
& jugged the hare in blood & butter.
Look, I said to a ring of children
& pointed. *It's gorgeous.*

DASH

Longer please! – two out of fifty usable words
you employ to hold us hostage –

longer in the cooling bath, longer
by the playground gates, mowing imaginary grass,

longer driving your car-cum-aeroplane –
and we want longer too –

and smaller boxes to fold your clothes into
or not to have to shed them at all –

but before we know what's hit us,
we're standing on the roadside, staring west

at the last of a trail of dust, like the crowds
who wait all day for a royal visit

for it to simply pass them by –
before they've memorised the hair, the eyes,

the inscrutable footmen, the marvellous horses

They're here to make money, the men distinguished
from the crowds they move among
by white hats and walking sticks,
to capture as many people as possible
for their fairground bioscope shows.
Come see yourselves on the screen as living history!

And history sets up its Nordenograph and rolls
and vacuums in the girls in shawls, the men and boys in caps,
the entire rollicking sea
of spinners and doffers and little tenters
departing the factory gates at six
like a nation's exodus.

Everyone wears clogs. Everyone has a dinner to get to.
But the dock of a quarter-day's pay for a minute of horseplay
is no longer over their heads
and so they jostle, momentarily, blurred face
by blurred face, to smile or to bow, for the transmission of grace
in the space near the cinematographer

as though the camera cast out a fraught pool of light
in exchange for their imprint
and they are standing in it.
The women loiter less. A handful of men doff caps, then laugh
or shake incredibly white, wide handkerchiefs
at whoever may prove their witness:

themselves, their wives, coal miners, tram conductors,
Boer War veterans, Lloyd George in the wings – who knows –
the King – not to mention the unthinkable yet-to-be-born,
not to mention me. And always, in every factory-gate frame,
like an offering up of driftwood

out of the indeterminate mass
after its comb and polish
or the crystallisation of salt from a smoky suspension,
children linger longest in the foreground,
shoving, lampooning, breaking the line,
or simply staring back at us, across the lens's promise,

as though we still held Passchendaele in our pockets
and could find a way to save them.
They grin and grin – *not yet, not yet* –
while in a corner of the screen, a cart horse stumbles,
flickers, flashes into darkness
where the cellulose nitrate stock rubbed off inside the milk churn.

SHADOWS IN SIBERIA ACCORDING TO KAPUŚCIŃSKI

Are upright –
cast not by sunlight but by frozen breath:

we breathe
and are enveloped in an outline

and when we pass,
this outline stays suspended, not tethered

to our ankles
as our sun-shadows are. A boy was here –

fantastically dressed
against the arctic frost like an heirloom glass

in bubble wrap –
he has disappeared into the portico

of himself. Not even Alice,
with her knack for finding weaknesses

in the shellac
of this world, left so deft a calling card.

from PARALLAX (2013)

1801

A beautiful cloudless morning. My toothache better.
William at work on The Pedlar. Miss Gell
left a basket of excellent lettuces; I shelled
our scarlet beans. Walked out after dinner for letters –
met a man who had once been a Captain begging for alms.

*

The afternoon airy & warm. No letters. Came home
via the lake, which was near-turquoise
& startled by summer geese.
The soles on this year's boots are getting worn.
Heard a tiny wounded yellow bird, sounding its alarm.

*

William as pale as a basin, exhausted with altering...
I boiled up pears with cloves.
Such visited evenings are sharp with love
I almost said *dear, look*. Either moonlight on Grasmere
                                        – like herrings! –
or the new moon holding the old moon in its arms.

BALTIMORE

In other noises, I hear my children crying –
in older children playing on the street
past bedtime, their voices buoyant
in the staggered light; or in the baby
next door, wakeful and petulant
through too-thin walls; or in the constant
freakish pitch of Westside Baltimore
on *The Wire*, its sirens and rapid gunfire,
its beleaguered cops haranguing kids
as young as six for propping up
the dealers on the corners, their swagger
and spitfire speech; or in the white space
between radio stations when no voice
comes at all and the crackling static
might be swallowing whole a child's
small call for help; even in silence itself,
its material loops and folds enveloping
a ghost cry, one I've made up, but heard,
that has me climbing the stairs, pausing
in the hall, listening, listening hard,
to – at most – rhythmical breathing
but more often than not to nothing, the air
of the landing thick with something missed,
dust motes, the overhang of blankets, a ship
on the Lough through the window, infant sleep.

SHOSTAKOVICH

The wind and its instruments were my secret teachers.
In Podolskaya Street I played piano for my mother
– note for note without a music sheet – while the wind
in the draughty flat kept up: tapping its fattened hand
against the glass, moaning through the stove, banging
a door repeatedly out on the landing –
the ghost in the machine of Beethoven's *Two Preludes
Through All the Major Keys*, that said they lied.

Later I stood in a wheat field and heard the wind make music
from everything it touched. The top notes were the husks:
fractious but nervous, giddy, little-voiced,
while underneath a strong strange melody pulsed
as though the grain was rigging, or a forest.

In all my praise and plainsong I wrote down
the sound of a man's boots from behind the mountain.

PHOTOGRAPHS OF BELFAST BY ALEXANDER ROBERT HOGG

The year the Great Ship Herself
is fitted out
at the mouth of the Lagan,

her panelling
drilled through and threaded
with miles of electric cables

and her gymnasium
horses finally bolted
down –

fifty cubic tonnes
of soot
falls over the city

in drifts, in rain, in air
breathed out then in again,
re-textured as dust.

He notices
the stark potential
of tarnished water

for the glass-plate photograph:
how there are slate tones
and oiliness together

and how, in standing pools
and running drains,
it coats the children's feet

with ubiquitous, gritty ink.
Alleyways and back yards
snag on his mind:

he can barely pass an entry
without assessing
the effect the diagonal

of a porterhouse roof
beside a streetlight
might produce, whereas

to photograph a yard
on Little York Street –
its ruin of toppled bricks

and broken guttering,
the windows of its houses,
open holes –

is to cast the viewer out
onto the no-man's-land
of her own estate

and to prove the eye is banked
as much by what unravels
as by flint.

There is the tidy shop
he makes his tidy living in
selling a wallet

of possible poses
for posterity: the Father
with his watch-chain,

the Sailor on his stool.
But for this commission
from the Corporation

he's sending home
dispatches from Sebastopol
Street in which

a man by the railings
ghosts himself
by turning his head too soon.

One cannot tell
if the room in the photograph
entitled *Number 36*

is inhabited –
light from the missing
upper storey is shafted

by jutting planks,
the fire-black walls
are crystalline

and yet outside similar terraces
with crumbling masonry
and dark for doors,

in bedraggled
unspeakable arcs
he's conjured with his shillings,

each child strong enough
to manage it
carries a child.

DISPLAY

movement is life

    – SLOGAN OF THE WOMEN'S LEAGUE OF HEALTH
    AND BEAUTY, 1930–1939

Hyde Park, 1936. Cold enough for scarves and hats
among the general populace, but not for the fifteen thousand women
from the League of Health and Beauty performing callisthenics
on the grass. It could be snowing, and they of Bromley-Croydon, Slough,
Glasgow, Belfast, would don no more than a pair of satin knickers
and a sleeveless satin vest to spin and stretch and bow
the body beautiful. Athens in London, under a sodden sky,
and Winnie and Molly and Doris metamorphosed.

On the edge of the revolving staves of arms and legs,
pale as comfrey – an army not yet on the move but almost ready –
there are tents for scones and tea. Kiddies, brought to watch
in caps and plaits, wriggle on deckchairs. Their mothers
carry vast, forbidden handbags on their laps and smell
of Lily of the Valley. All around the periphery,
in huddled clumps of overcoats and smoke,
from offices and railway yards, men joke and talk, gesticulate –

but mostly they just look, quietly and sharply focused,
like eyeing up the horses at a racecourse, but with much more choice.
For those crammed in steaming picturehouses later, a commentator,
brusquely charmed, declares *the perfection of British womanhood:
to them belongs the future!* – while the ghost of Mary Bagot Stack,
whose dream this is, smiles back. Their hair cut short, slim,
co-ordinated as the League of German Maidens or a chorus set
from Hollywood, fit for birth, the women twirl and kick,

do foot-swings and scissor-jacks, link hands or fall
suddenly flat as pegs in a collapsible building, then bounce back
up again, for movement is life and they are keeping moving.
To hell with it, they may as well be saying. Twist.
To hell with Lizzie Evans and her bitching hate.
With blood and vinegar. With getting in the tin bath last.
With laddered stockings. With sore wrists at the factory.
I've got the fresh-air-body they promised me. Twist. Its electricity.

FUR

At 25 and 29 respectively, Hans Holbein's
burly furred ambassadors haven't got long to go:
the pox, the plague, the ague, a splinter
in the finger, a scratch at the back of the throat
or an infection set into the shoulder joint
might carry them off, in a matter of writhing
hours, at any instant –

                    Too obvious a touch

to set the white skull straight.   Better
to paint it as something other: driftwood
up-ended by magic from the right-hand side
of the tesserae carpet; to let it hang
like an improbable boomerang just under
the clutch of pipes, the lute with the broken
string, still casting a shadow...

For there is bewitchery in those brown beards yet –
in the (slightly) rakish tilt to the saucer hat
of the ambassador on the left.

A DAY'S BLINDNESS

December. The year at the back of it
blown and shrunk to dark
in the morning, dark in the afternoon
and the light in between
like the pale blue flicker of a pilot light
in a boiler's black intestine.

There was the usual breakfast
– coffee, soda bread, jam –
neither one of them speaking.
Her slept-on hair. The papers
still to go out for and a walk
to the top of the road and back,

past crows' nests fisted in trees,
to look at the Lough. It happened
at once: no jolt, no warning,
no shutter cranking low
over everything, no shadows
starting off on the periphery

like hares in fields
then gradually thickening.
He stood up to carry his plate and cup
to the sink and couldn't see.
He sat back down. The clocks
went on consuming Saturday.

He would have needed practice
at being blind to pretend to be sighted.
He had none, so she saw.
The son was away in Florida.
He asked her to leave, and for hours then,
as through the womb's wall,

he heard her about the house,
moving around upstairs,
using the bathroom, and perhaps
just once – or twice? –
saying something soft
and incoherent into the telephone.

Outside, at a quarter to four,
a watery sunset broke over
the squat hills. He couldn't tell
the lifting and the thud
of the returning dark apart.
He sat on at the table,

rolling crumbs beneath his thumbs
and waiting, either for what was taken
to be handed back –
the fridge, the kettle, his cuff-linked shirt –
or for the kleptomaniac visitor
he couldn't lock out

to be done with it, finally,
to sever the link –
to haul him up out of his chair,
into the hall, and through the brown door
to a garden ruined with hooves
and there would be

horses set loose from the Bond Yard
where his father worked
in the Hungry Thirties,
their coats engrained with soot
and their heads encased in steam,
accusing him.

The Royal children have been sent a gift –
A map of Europe from 1766
Complete with longitude, painted onto wood,
Like any other map in brown and green and red,
But then disfigured: cut up into parts,
A disassembly of tiny courts
Strewn across the table. There is a key
To help the children slot, country by country,
The known traversable world in place:
Little Tartary, Swedish Lapland, France,
The Government of Archangel. The sea
Has been divided into squares, crudely,
As though the cast-iron sides of nations
Still applied (but with more attention
To geometry) while the engraver's signature
– A circle, his name, a folded flower –
Has been deftly sawn in half. If successful,
The three young princes and the oldest girl
(This is not, after all, a lesson in diplomacy
So she can play too) will, ironically,
Undo the puzzle's title and its claim:
Europe Divided in its Kingdoms
Shall be Europe reconfigured, whole.
They start in the top left corner with the scale
Then fill the other corners in: 'Part of Africa',
A scroll, the blank of simply 'Asia'
Rolling off to hordes and steppes and snow
Beyond the boundary. Outlines follow,
Aided by exquisite lettering:

'The Frozen Ocean' solidifies across the map's ceiling...
And so the Royal children spend an hour
Staring and exclaiming, clicking together
(What joy!) the angled buttress of a continent –
Their own unlikely island on a slant
By its farthest edge, and in their trance ignore
What will no longer fit: Aotearoa, America.

PUZZLE

for Sheila Llewellyn

Vitya pledges his brigade of Pioneers will plant
half as many fruit trees as the other Pioneers.
Kiryusha pledges *his* brigade, the best of the detachment,
will match the trees of all brigades together, including Vitya's.
Their brigades work the last shift simultaneously.
The preceding brigades of the detachment
plant forty trees. Both pledges are fulfilled exactly.
How many trees does the whole detachment plant?

Answer: a kind of Latin, finished and intricate,
or a box of glass-plate negatives from 1887
unearthed by accident of Newcastle Cloth Market.
The Oceanic Whitetip Shark. Ectoplasm.
Natasha Ivanova on her collective farm
working out the most efficient way to harvest cotton.

PHOTOGRAPHING LOWRY'S HOUSE

And then he died.
And so I drove to where
he'd lived. I don't know why.
To stand across the street,
perhaps, hands in my pockets,
a happenstance observer

of the bricks, the Georgian
front, the chimney pots
and guttering, the bin,
the hedge, the fence,
appearing all-at-once
untenanted, bereft –

to take a photograph
or two of how that looked.
But his house was a smashed
hive, all industry and ruin:
the door was open;
vans with their backs

thrown wide cluttered
the driveway; men he never knew
in life were loading up
painting after painting –
portraits, landscapes, mill-scenes –
stripping every room

of his obsessions.
And so I intervened, crying theft
and history, and they listened.
And I was given half
an hour to photograph
what was left

before they finished.
Light inside the hallway,
even in February: without a flash
the staircase seeming flounced
in the train of a bridal dress,
shimmery

as the white space
in the foreyards of the factories
his buckled, blank-faced
people bent their bodies to.
The mantelpiece in the living-room
strewn with stories –

postcards, knick-knacks,
impromptu napkin sketches;
the bar-talk of the clocks,
each set to a different time
in case their simultaneous chimes
distressed him; likenesses

of his parents scowling down.
But as though I stood in Lascaux
among its sprinting fawns
and my very breath
was wrecking what I stared at,
there were absences also:

squares of thin-lined stains
where, moments earlier,
pictures in their frames
had kept their residence –
impossible now to distinguish
which. My camera

clicked and whirled.
Upstairs I found his studio.
I changed the film.
They'd been in here
but not for long – everywhere,
archipelagos

of canvases he'd lain
against the window or the walls
still held their chains.
Persons, closer up than anything
of his I'd ever seen:
a boy and girl,

huddled and lovely
against a fogged-out background;
a man and his family,
everyone in it
round-shouldered and perplexed
by being found;

a child hitching a lift
in a barrow. And then the sea,
over and over: with a black ship
smoking into harbour,
or a distraction of yachts, or
waves and horizon only –

de-peopled, the tide
that one day didn't turn
but swallowed
the cacophony
of Salford and Pendlebury
and kept on coming on.

I had a minute
in the bedroom with Rossetti's
luscious women, standing silent
guard about his bed.
The counterpane re-made.
And then the foreman called me

from the first-floor landing –
they had to be getting on,
I should be going – and I had time
for a final shot
on my botched way out:
his trilby and his mac, hanging

from a hook, in black and white.

DAUGHTER

after Robert Pinsky

I

She wakes at 7am –
her internal clock
unstintingly accurate –
and can sleep twelve hours
at a stretch without
losing hold of her last thought.
The grievance she fell
asleep with: *you didn't*
get me rice milk or
you didn't sing me
song 'bout Tommy Thumb –
her dawn declaration.
Though she'll also ask
is it morning?
just to check
she hasn't missed
the best and purest
portion of her day, the bit
with her brother and breakfast
in it, by being away.

11

The dresses and tops
in her wardrobe
smell of fabric conditioner –
sugar, vanilla, baking soda –
and are frequently washed.
The clothes she harries
off and leaves in heaps
on stairs and sofas
so she can flash
about the house
with nothing on –
a moon-pale, decelerating
balloon – recall whiskey:
layered, earthy, consisting
of neither sweat nor
excrement but of what
her deeper body's left
behind itself in warmth.
I cannot tell the strands
of it apart.

III

Cut off by the Atlantic,
half her family
are permanently absent
though she hasn't
noticed this yet.
Her world is still
the roof over 'safe'
in the Japanese pictograph.
Her fiercest, non-human
attachments are to
vibrantly coloured objects
– orange plate, red fork –
she cannot eat without.
She's learning this house
like a psalm: the crack
in the kitchen sink,
the drawers and all
their warring contents,
the geography of each room
immutable as television.

IV

When visitors come
she's keen to show them
the most horrific thing
she knows: Rien Poortvliet's
picture of a Snotgurgle
in the *Bantam Book of Gnomes*.
Scabrous, radically
lopsided, huge –
he's forcing a gnome
through a mangle
while his sidekick black
rat laughs. The book
falls open at his face.
She might be Persephone,
bravely showing off
what she's survived,
but it's probably the snot
she's more delighted by:
the viscous, glittering rivulets
he hasn't wiped away.

V

In Timothy Leary's
eight-circuit system
of human evolution
there's a drug for every stage.
Acquiring language
or the Symbol State
(concerning itself with maps
and artefacts) is mimicked
by amphetamines:
crystal meth, benzedrine.
Silent too long as an infant,
our daughter talks all day –
her toys, her toes,
her pictures, her minutely
attenuated hierarchy
of friends –
like a businessman
on the last train home
after one too many espressos,
selling you his dream.

A MATTER OF LIFE AND DEATH

On the afternoon I'm going into labour so haltingly it's still easy
　　to bend and breathe, bend and breathe, each time the erratic clamp
　　　　sets its grip about my pelvis, then releases –

I take a nap, eat lunch and while you pen a letter to our impending offspring
　　explaining who we are, what there is on offer in the house
　　　　we don't yet know we'll leave, to be handed over

on his eighteenth birthday like a key to the demesne, sit front-to-back
　　on an upright chair in the living-room and switch on the television.
　　　　World War II. David Niven is faltering after a bombing op

in a shot-up plane. *Conservative by nature, Labour by conviction,*
　　he quotes Sir Walter Raleigh: *O give me my scallopshell of quiet,*
　　　　my staff of faith to walk upon, while a terrified American radio girl

listens in. It's all fire and ravenous engine noise – he can't land
　　because the fuselage is damaged and he hasn't a parachute.
　　　　Then, because *he'd rather fall than fry,* he bales out anyway –

a blip on the screen vanishing into cloud cover. The girl hides her face in her hands.
　　The baby drops a fraction of an inch and the next contraction hurts.
　　　　I know I'm at the gentlest end of an attenuated scale

of pain relief: climbing the stairs, a bath, two aspirin, tapering down as the hours
　　roll on (and we relocate to hospital) to gas and air, pethidine,
　　　　a needle in the spine, and go out to walk the sunny verges

of our cul-de-sac like a wind-up, fat-man toy, tottering every five minutes or so
　　into a bow. Nobody's home. The bins are still out on the road
　　　　after this morning's pick-up. The light is slant and filled

with running gold. Back inside, the film has switched to Technicolor
    monochrome: an anachronistic afterlife in grey in which dead airmen
        sign in under 'name' and 'rank', the Yanks smack gum

and swagger, *isn't this swell?* and a legion of otherworldly women
    with hair rolled high as dunes hand out enormous plaster wings
        to the just-deceased. The dead are invoiced for,

like battleships or teapots, their names on the list ticked off
    as they swing through each allotted doorway clean and whole
        and orderly – the incomprehensible machinery of life and death

a question of books that balance. And there's this sudden tug inside,
    rigging straining taut and singing, and I cry out for the first time,
        and in you come to coax and soothe as though I'm *doing* something –

running a marathon, climbing a mountain – instead of being forced back down
    into my seat by some psychopathic schoolmarm over and over again,
        stay. And I think of my granny and her *forty-six hours*

of agony, shifting my mother from one world to the next, and how that birth
    cut short her happiness at the Raleigh bicycle factory in Nottingham
        where her youth was spent in *secret war work*, typing up invoices.

Back in heaven, there's about as much commotion as there's been in a million
    years (a slight shake of the head by the woman in charge, a sigh)
        because David Niven, who should have arrived but hasn't,

landed on a beach and – how? – survived, met the American radio operator
    as she cycled home after the night-shift, and fell in love. He must be sent for.
        Down below, they're already looking post-coital: picnicking in civvies

on a homespun Tartan rug in a Technicolor rose garden. I'm not supposed
     to show up at the hospital for hours, or not until the cervix
          has done its slow, industrial cranking-wide enough to be marked

by a thumb-span, and the problem is I don't know what that means, or how to tell,
     or how much worse the pain is going to get (answer: a lot)
          and so the afternoon grows hot and narrow and you abandon

your confessions altogether and the botched clock of paradise with seven hands
     across its face ticks on the wall. *I've seen it many times*, said my granny,
          when a new life comes into a family, an old life goes out –

as though there were checks and balances, birth weighted against death
     like a tidy invoice, and a precise amount of room allotted the living.
          Before we inch upstairs to the bathroom to test what sweet relief

is granted, after all, by a bath and lavender oil, I catch sight of a
     magical marble escalator – the original stairway to heaven – with David Niven
          captive on its steps being hauled away to the sound of a clanking bell

from his radiant girlfriend, and I imagine my granny, who died three weeks ago
     on a hospital ward in Chesterfield, *making room* as she herself predicted,
          not dumb and stricken and hollowed out with cancer

but young, glamorous, childless, free, in her 1940s' shoes and sticky lipstick,
     clicking about the office of new arrivals as though she owns it,
          flicking open the leather-bound ledger and asking him to sign.

THE DOCTORS

to blurt it out like a Polaroid
PAUL MULDOON

In this country
they are desecrating photographs –
those that tell the truth of their own flown moment
simply as it was, that are naïve as schoolchildren
set down in a bewildering classroom and bid to speak
their name and place of birth in a foreign tongue,
who revert, instinctively, to their own, as slates
and straps and canes rain down upon them.

It is the camera's
inherent generosity of outlook
which is more often than not at fault:
the one-whose-name-we-dare-not-whisper
sitting at breakfast with Our Great Leader
on holiday in the Urals, or idly grinding his teeth
in a dim committee room, his glasses like miniature
headlights reflecting the flash.

With scissors,
nail files, ink and sellotape, he has been vanished –
alongside other party operatives who touched
His sleeve, or didn't clap for long enough, or loved
their wives, or laughed, or who pointed the way
down some rickety steps as though He needed help
– whole politburos cropped to a man, or at most
a handful of survivors ranged around a chess table,

scratched absences
over their shoulders made luminous as moons.
It is addictive: the urge to utter a language
both singular and clean. It is progressive –
how the power to transform a conspirator into a pillar
transmutes, in turn, to the eradication
of the accidental as a class of photograph:
how litter, bleak weather, a sneer,

or too many smiling
parents who later disappeared are also doctored.
And should anyone be missed – turning up
in textbooks before the grave extent
of their transgression's been established –
a nation's girls and boys, all trained
in proper parlance, their fingers stained with soot,
draw over women's faces black balloons.

LIGHTHOUSE

My son's awake at ten, stretched out along
his bunk beneath the ceiling, wired and watchful.
The end of August. Already the high-flung
daylight sky of our Northern solstice dulls
earlier and earlier to a clouded bowl;
his Star of David lamp and plastic moon
have turned the dusk to dark outside his room.

Across the Lough, where ferries venture blithely
and once a cruise ship, massive as a palace,
inched its brilliant decks to open sea –
a lighthouse starts its own nightlong address
in fractured signalling; it blinks and bats
the swingball of its beam, then stands to catch,
then hurls it out again beyond its parallax.

He counts each creamy loop inside his head,
each well-black interval, and thinks it just for him –
this gesture from a world that can't be entered:
the two of them partly curtained, partly seen,
upheld in a sort of boy-talk conversation
no one else can hear. That private place, it answers,
with birds and slatted windows – I've been there.

THE MUTOSCOPE

Double Trouble, The Ghost Café, Late at Night
in the Bedroom: each Mutoscope tells its story
to whoever steps right up, drops a penny in its slot

and cranks the handle. Mimicking decency,
the poster shows a solid Victorian gentlewoman
stooping to its glass as though sniffing narcissi

in a window box, her hat a fountain.
A World of Moving Pictures, Very Popular
in Public Places, it is, in fact, an intimate machine

whose jittery flickerings of marital war,
a monkey on a bicycle, or a lady being undressed
from a through-the-keyhole, what-the-butler-saw

perspective, no one else can watch
at the same time. Sir or Madam, yours is the hand
that squares the frame, undoes the catch

at the top of the reel and sets eight hundred
separate photographs tumbling into blackness
against a brown-paper background

but showing you each shot before they vanish.
Only for you do the two mute girls on stage
who falter at first, erratic as static

in the synaptic gap between each image,
imperceptibly jolt to life –
grinning, tap-dancing, morphing into footage,

their arms like immaculate pistons, their legs like knives…
It lasts a minute, their having-been-written onto light.

Ingrid in her shawl's been here since nine,
burdening the tables on loan
from the church downstairs with Babushka dolls
and caviar, handkerchiefs and wine

from Yugoslavia, Bulgarian perfume.
My brother and I ask for a job
and are handed pink and white posters
of *Peace & Détente* to decorate the room.

It's trickier than we thought
to stick them straight so secretly we give up.
Almost everyone's smoking.
In the background, *Kalinka* on cassette

belted out by the Red Army Choir
wobbles towards its peak. There's tea,
coffee, Irish stew, and a cool display
of anti-Mrs Thatcher paraphernalia –

pens in the shape of nails for her coffin
we'll buy and use in school.
Shop stewards come, and sympathisers
who, once a year, like Christians,

demonstrate their faith, the odd
bewildered lured-in shopper looking for soap,
or socks, but mostly it's just us:
Card Carriers and the Kids Thereof,

filling up the air with fevered talk. By four,
Rosemary Street's ablaze in the solstice dark.
We pack what's left of the wooden trains and vodka
into crates for another year and repair

to the Duke of York, where once
an actual Soviet Representative – tall, thin –
in frost-inflected English gave a speech,
and I clutched my lemonade and was convinced.

A LIE

That their days were not like our days,
the different people who lived in sepia –

more buttoned, colder, with slower wheels,
shut off, sunk back in the unwakeable house

for all we call and knock. And even the man
with the box and the flaming torch

who made his servants stand so still
their faces itched can't offer us what it cost

to watch the foreyard being lost
to cream and shadow, the pierced sky

placed in a frame. Irises under the windowsill
were the colour of Ancient Rome.

BLOG

I don't have girlfriends but I do have sex
with a different woman about three times a month.
Sometimes more. Sometimes less. I rarely ask.

They'll stop to talk to me in the supermarket
or on the bus. Off-handedly at first.
They're not made-up or drunk. We don't flirt

or analyse it. There's this tiny electrical thrill
gets passed like an egg-yolk slipping
between the cups of its own split shell.

They take me home. It happens. I leave. Simple.
They don't invite me to dinner or text.
It's easy and clean and consensual.

Then it happens again. Loneliness's overblown –
unless I'm just one of the unnaturally blessed.
My good friend Jack told me to write this down.

DON JUAN, 2012

And Money, that most pure imagination...
– Don Juan, Canto XII, 2, 7

I

We need a hero. The time is out of joint,
  has burnt its fragile socket, while for the Mayans,
who read their dazzling mountain stars like newsprint,
  transcribing mankind's pre-allotted lifespan –
by 2012, there's simply no more of it.
  God's eighteenth-century clock has winded down.
We're at the end, or so the websites warn us,
of everything we know and value precious.

I'm usually unconvinced, convinced instead
  that end-of-history talk is soon demolished
by history's own refusal to be led
  into some silent terminus. Things may not flourish:
we may be colder, hungrier, more upset
  by the growing list of what's been taken from us.
But even lame, thin, choking and at variance
with the riches of before, we'll falter on regardless.

Now I'm not so sure. Take this week's news:
  a cataclysm, a herculean
storm unlike anything even Al Gore lent shape to
  is closing in, caused partly by a shifting jet-stream,
partly by the pole-ice melting through –
  a rough beast rising as the oceans warm.
We watch its blue-white swirl by satellite
on flashy CNN, like spies on our own planet.

We watch it hit. They've timed it to the second.
    A waterproofed and clearly mad reporter
getting tossed across a junction by the wind,
    then back again, up to his calves in water,
tries to speak to us but his voice is drowned.
    The anchorwoman smiles and leaves him there,
shuttling between the leaning trees and the signals
as the rain rolls over him and the picture fails.

By morning we're in Aftermath, a birdseye view:
    parks and streets submerged in the ravaged cities –
sheets of pewter sea blown into a new,
    transplanted element; kilometres of débris.
The northeast national grid has blown its fuse.
    The graces we now live by – transport, electricity –
that house us all in rooms of heated glass
lie savaged and defunct as the cable telegraph.

And how much will it cost? Dear Lord, the cost...
    Tens of billions, according to the *Guardian*,
on insurance claims alone for what's been lost.
    Since the financial crisis, we can't imagine
what so many profligate zeros, nestled close,
    reproduced like cells, have come to *mean* –
they march across our headlines, black and crass,
and always with a minus sign attached.

A little while ago in Houston Texas
	three awfully clever men invented something
very bold and deft and half-miraculous:
	a fresh, *creative* way to run accounting
(and why not?) whereby losses make a plus.
	They made wealth up: income, future earnings,
so that, sign without a signifier, wild
in its own unfettered realm, money multiplied...

...until it crashed. O what a falling off!
	While thousands lost their pensions, they went to jail
in handcuffs, though sadly not for long enough,
	and not before their brainchild had gone viral.
Soon debt became a bargainable stock
	and the trick with debt, how it loves to dive and spiral,
a ballooning asset. Champagne baths on Wall Street,
	the fizz of endless cash and nothing cheap,

not even escorts, a 'legitimate' expense,
	and certainly not the cars, the drugs, accessories
for adventure sports, the loft apartments.
	But holes are holes, no matter how unholily
they may be cloaked with crafty argument,
	and Enron's falling off just mere pinprickery
compared to the current void. A chasm splits
the contours of the earth. We're staring into it.

Like Attack of the Giant Crabs! The Killer Spiders!
   (small and normal creatures malformed by radiation)
all the hidden less-than-zero numbers,
   tired of being barred, like ruined cousins,
from civilised conversation, staged a takeover.
   We're starving, they announced, *and we are Legion.*
The mega-banks went first: their secret debts
devoured them from within, then spat them out.

The other banks we salvaged with our taxes.
   And for what? Their doors stay double-bolted
while talk of what we haven't got in practice
   is all the rage since money's lack revolted.
Nothing's offered: no credit, ready cash,
   no sweet forgiving margin; those evicted
from the homes they can't afford, who bought too late,
live someplace other than on ghost estates.

The outlook's bleak. We're inside a climacteric
   our baby-boomer parents never dreamt of
who grew up in the groove of post-war pop music,
   who always had a job, who shared their love.
As weather forecasts grow apocalyptic,
   as doubting politicians lose their nerve,
as markets tumble, as what we're told we'll owe
engulfs our children's children – we need a hero.

II

A Judge? A Pope? A President? Not likely.
   Four years ago we thought we'd found a true one
when Obama won the White House. His wife was pretty,
   his daughters tall and modest; his speeches shone
like electroplated costume jewellery
   with glittering abstract nouns: *justice, freedom...*
But the poetry of campaigning got rearranged
as prose once he took office. Little changed.

Someone close to power but not wet-through
   with it; someone honest, wry, congenial,
who's commonplace enough to not be deaf to
   the voice of that most abstract noun, the people.
No banking magnate, no plane-and-shipping guru,
   no prophet of a lizard nation, no angel –
but best of all a mirror or a silver screen
we catch our captured selves reflected in.

Enter Donald Johnson. At sixty-three
   childless, virile, handsome, single, rich
with all the things he's done and where he's been
   (Australia, Budapest), still sleek and boyish,
still dynamic, still brim-full of bewitchery
   with women (who are still the ones to ravish
him) and who has recently found employment
as an attaché in the European Parliament.

To such a skilled adventurer, Belgium is dull
    (with compensations: waffles, chocolates, beer
so fine he quaffs it by the tankardful,
    mussels steamed in wine, shallots and butter,
stupendous *frites*) but on the whole he's grateful –
    a job's a job and he isn't getting younger.
He has a tiny flat above a park
and visits, *le weekend, Les Museés des Beaux-Arts.*

Work's a doddle. The mechanics of the Union
    grind and turn, down miles of spotless corridors
in countless shiny rooms. A gravy train
    for every sort of bureaucrat: directors,
policy advisors, inventors of Eurojargon
    (*Flexicurity, Acquis Communautaire*),
advocacy officers. The EU's sound:
it's well-oiled and its wheels go round and round.

He breakfasts with the Secretary at nine.
    He de-briefs after meetings those beneath him.
He drafts agendas, often before the deadline.
    He sets up conference calls in French and German.
He tracks reports and checks if stats align
    with various previous member-state projections.
He leaves at ten, to dine and then to bed
sometimes alone and sometimes with a friend.

And then things change. The map is not the territory
   and metaphor, like language, leaves a gap
between the thing described and its new summary.
   So when things change, metaphor plays catch-up.
A greased machine? The EU-as-a-Body's
   more apt now its economies are crap;
it ate a lot, in what they termed 'expansion',
then instantly fell foul of such infection

it threatens to expire... The US sneezed,
   the EU caught the flu: national debts
so vast (and growing) they betray disease,
   rising unemployment, frozen assets,
tottering banks and shrinking GDPs.
   The five most gangrenous toes on Europe's foot –
Ireland, Italy, Portugal, Spain and Greece –
are losing blood and blackening from necrosis.

Surgeons stand ready, scrubbed and dressed in green.
   Austerity! Austerity! – the answer
backed by Merkel, Europe's undisputed Sovereign –
   has gripped us all ('we're all in this together')
but is gripping some like a slip-knot at a hanging.
   Austerity the 'Fury' with 'abhorrèd shears'
who 'slits the thin-spun life' – the dreadful price –
the cutting off the nose to save the face...

It's Monday morning, dim with Brussels rain.
   November 12th. The Secretary's serious.
He doesn't want to deal with the campaign
   on Donald's list (a biodiversity crisis)
and stares into his coffee. News in from Spain
   is dire, but the news from Greece disastrous
as Austerity cuts deep, cuts deeper still...
He wants a witness, someone with the skill

of staying low, anonymous and watchful,
   to gather notes and keep him up to date
on how the current measures have proved harmful
   (beyond the TV, papers and debates
in the two parliaments) to 'ordinary people'.
   He spreads his hands. 'I'd like to delegate
this research trip to *you*, Mr Johnson.'
Call it a hero's quest, call it a mission –

Donald coughs and nods. Outside the window
   cherry trees in rows are almost bare:
the last of their scarlet/golden leaves to go
   before the winter, flash their burnished fire.
His ticket's booked. He'll leave for Greece tomorrow.
   The bleeding South. He's never been before
(but knows Lord Byron died there). He thinks of sun
and olives, wine with resin... Revolution.

III

Brussels' airport's busy with arrivals –
    a crisis brings the margins to the Centre
like supplicants to Rome. Its polished hall
    of cafés gleams and hums. Spice-in-sugar:
the caffeinated jazz of morning travel
    sets Donald tingling. He buys cologne, saunters
towards his departure gate, checks his watch,
then thinks of white geese ranged around a trough

with held-back wings as he stares at the jets outside.
    Hardly anyone's flying to Greece. No tourists.
No families steering buggies loaded high
    with snacks and nappies. No propertyists.
A bored EU official scans the sky;
    another suffers questions from a journalist
and by the entrance, a woman on her own
stands scrolling through a document by smartphone.

Donald looks again. Too long ago
    an interpreter for Russian sent a text
which conjured up the dear, well-worn scenario:
    dinner, drinks, a so-what-happens-next...?
Perhaps a month. He mouths a warm hello
    across the seats, but she only seems perplexed
and looks away. She's dark, composed, allusive.
This only serves to make her more attractive.

The cabin's almost empty. Mozart trills
   to a frothy, crested peak – and down again.
Scattered heads observe the safety drill.
   Then the roar and lift of flight, the seat-belt sign
clicks off, and she's suddenly beside him in the aisle,
   asking if she can join him. Donald feigns
surprise and says of course. Not *over*-gleefully.
She stretches out her hand. 'I'm Persephone.'

She stows her laptop, feathers out her hair.
   He asks her if she makes this journey often.
She turns her gaze to his. 'Once a year.'
   They order wine – a lull before the conversation
loosens its tie and runs. 'Every winter,
   from November to February. I live in Athens.
And you, Mr...?' 'Johnson. Call me Donald. Please.'
All is good. The flight's as smooth as a Baileys;

clouds are massed like floss beneath the wing-tip;
   sun is streaming in; she's friendly, smart,
with brilliant teeth and slightly glossy lips
   and could sweeten, not just the clockwork start
to this morning's flight but the whole damn trip...
   He muses on seduction, its lines, its parts,
its dartings forth, its keeping some things buried,
and mentally marks a tick for 'clearly interested'

as he listens to her talk. She talks a lot.
    And so the game of Working-Out commences.
She laughs and volunteers that she's a Eurocrat:
    a Master's in economics, fluent French,
a decade's stellar service (which makes her what,
thirty-five or -six? – not, he thinks, on balance,
disturbingly his junior) and sent to oversee,
each winter, changes to the EU C.A.P.

in her own benighted country, on which she's expert.
    She wears no ring. 'It must be hard on your husband
when you leave?' She shrugs. 'He tolerates it:
    since we met, it's just what's always happened.
We lead our Belgian life, easy, quiet –
    not volatile, not raw-edged or impassioned –
and then I'm gone, and our winter lives are different
and we never ask precisely how they're spent.'

A husband – damn. But O the little thud
    in Donald's groin as she scurries to dispel him!
She's said enough, she's said more than she should
    if Donald doesn't rush to state his freedom
just as obviously. The flurry in his blood
    engulfs his knees. Is it the Sauvignon?
Is it the sun-drenched cloud-scape for a view?
He turns to her directly. 'I want you –'

and there's a moment then – she holds his stare,
    not moving, calm – and he listens to the engine
through the floor, and feels the pulse of her,
    as though they'd touched already, as though she'd spun
a web of silk and drawn him in. He falters,
    flutters closer (her mouth is slightly open)
and they kiss: a single quivering kiss,
and he's weirdly trapped like a climber in a crevice

as something rank runs through him, something cold
    from caverns too long shut to wind and light
deep inside the ground, where little grows
    but the thousand-year-long creep of stalactites
and fishless rivers carve out limestone folds
    and viaducts, and nameless shapes take flight –
He pulls away. The world is bright and stable:
here are his hands, here is his tray-table,

there's a suited woman smiling her assent,
    looking (slightly) embarrassed by his haste
but not affronted; they've started their descent.
    The seat-belt sign clicks on. 'That's a foretaste,'
she offers softly. Then she gathers her equipment
    and is gone – as though he's dreamt her face,
her lips, the untold clammy depths of her...
Her perfume fills the air. Donald shudders.

IV

What is it we fear? We fear the loss
    of whatever it is we've set about our hearths
to keep life's slicing cold at bay: a house;
    a food supply; coins that hold their worth
from one day to the next; a health service.
    We fear the loss of a perpetually generous Earth.
We fear the end of buses, the closure of stores,
we fear a return to conditions between the wars

when ragged men in lines brought all they owned –
    a battered bowl and spoon – to public kitchens;
when governments were fractured, jelly-boned,
    and hostage to a mass, enraged sedition
that ushered in such darkness, light was doomed.
    We fear a return to the Old Road into London
where mothers left their babies in their hundreds
to die of cold and lack of Parish funds.

In 2012, on the 13th of November,
    all over Greece – in Athens, on the islands,
in the agricultural north – Loss is Ruler
    and only the slick and sheltered rich withstand
its hunger. Every flat, every schoolyard and taverna
    plays its host, and should the honeyed
Sirens still exist, their singing would be rent
with Greece's wailing, and turn into lament.

The airport's crazy. Just the day before
   a budget slashing billions, yet again,
from salaries and services was deplored
   around the Chamber, then passed by a squeaky margin.
Another national strike looms like a downpour.
   The rush to leave in advance of a total shut-down
is panic-stricken. Donald doesn't feel well.
He takes a taxi to a moderate hotel,

showers, cleans his teeth, and falls asleep
   in a room that's beige and redolent with smoke
and dreams a lake. He's standing ankle-deep
   and then he's flailing underwater and he chokes
and then he stops. He looks. Trapped – in reeds –
   a long-haired, staring girl... He jolts awake.
Outside on the street, two men are arguing.
Their voices play like scales: rising, falling,

rising... It doesn't end. The clock says eight –
   he thought it would be earlier but the difference
in the hour? How did he sleep so late?
   The room is dark. Headlights' luminescence
moves around the walls. He needs to eat,
   shake off the wide-eyed girl, experience
the city in the evening, start making notes...
He stows his wallet and his phone inside his coat,

ignores the lift, trips down the dusty stairs,
    and is in the lobby, striding towards the exit,
when he sees her – straight-backed in an armchair,
    waiting. She's changed: no longer in a suit
but in a dress, not wearing make-up, older.
    He'd told her nothing, now he thinks of it:
nothing about his life, his job, the reason
for the trip. Did she *follow* him?

'Mr Johnson –' She's stood to stop him leaving.
    He brushes past. 'I'm here to introduce
you to the current facts. My car is waiting.'
    And the strangeness of the day – its working loose
of steady, regular stuff (read *sleep* and *kissing*)
    like a tongue around a half-extracted tooth –
goes up one notch. He finds himself disarmed,
inside her car as the door is being slammed,

Persephone beside him in the back,
    a wordless driver skulking in the front,
the night, both brightly lit and densely black,
    unravelling by his window, and what he wants
to say – *how dare you* – vanishing like a snowflake
    on a spit. He tries to speak but can't.
Athens seems normal: lovers hand-in-hand;
illuminated bars; tobacco stands –

like any typical European capital
    with tree-lined avenues of modern flats;
market squares packed tight with canvas stalls;
    displays of jewels and shoes and sequinned hats
gleaming in the darkness; a City Hall
    fronted by gushing fountains. Though there are rats:
he spots one as they angle round a corner,
flashed up by the headlights, then another –

then another – fast and fat and freakish –
    running out of pipes or into drains –
the streets are twitching. Tottering piles of rubbish
    begin to catch his eye. They turn again
into a major thoroughfare. He hadn't noticed,
    but garbage bags are everywhere: thrown
in heaps round litter bins, clogging doorways –
the refuse of a city, left for days...

'Welcome to the Winter of our Discontent.
    It's lasted years but now it's getting worse.
We borrow double, for every Euro spent.
    There's a bottomless pit in place of the public purse
that can't be filled, though each successive government
    tries its best. This is our constant curse,
like Sisyphus.' Sirens tear the air.
She leans forward in her seat. 'Syntagma Square.'

V

Syntagma Square, Syntagma Square's on fire
   Boots and batons, petrol bombs and bricks
They've strung up Merkel's portrait on a wire
   They've burned the German flag for bitter kicks
They've dumped the Euro symbol on the pyre
   and asked police to suck their fucking pricks
It's blazing, it's amazing, it's a whirl
with teargas and cannons, down in the underworld –

What do you get if you slice a loaf in half,
   then half, then half again? Answer: hungry.
What do you get if you lay off half your staff,
   the public civil servants of your country,
then threaten to axe the rest? Wheat from chaff,
   or the sudden, icy plunge into 'mere anarchy'?
You face two doors: an 'out'-door and an 'in'-door;
their signs are hidden, but both of them are trapdoors –

Eight little Indians, gayest under heaven –
   (seven little Indians, chopping up sticks)
one went to sleep, then there were seven –
   (one chopped himself in half and then there were six)
And there's never any chance of getting even
   And the wings to lift you out of here are wax –
One little Indian, left all alone,
he went out and hanged himself and then there were none –

The roar increases. A camera crew retreats.
 The riot squad advances like a wall.
Huddled against Persephone, Donald sweats.
 He doesn't want to stay with her at all
but there's smoke and screaming out there on the streets
 and he doesn't know the way to his hotel...
As though she's made her point (or read his mind),
she clears her throat, the car backs round a bend

then screeches off, untouched. They roll along
 past empty restaurants, strings of shuttered shops,
an ambulance growing fainter like a song
 on a turned-down radio, until it stops.
Persephone says: 'Disorder will go on –
 they'll broadcast it as students versus cops –
but it's everyone. The people have no choice.
They're damned already.' Donald finds his voice:

'Where are we headed to next?' 'A quiet place –'
 (O the relief of that!) –' to a garden.'
They're there in minutes: a residential space
 between two railway lines, overgrown
with weeds and shards and dubious sorts of waste –
 the kind of neglected by-pass, gypsy-rotten,
where immigrants begin their new existence
overlooked by us. Except there's silence:

no lights on in the flats; no signs of cooking;
   no children on the swing that someone's improvised;
no beat-up vans or bikes, no tethered washing.
   'Who were they?' 'These were Syrians, terrorised
by Assad, and his overindulged-in bombing
   of hospitals and schools. But Greece is immunised –
Europe's most porous border no longer leaks:
we round them up and house them all in concrete,

thirty to a cell – Iraqis, Afghans –
   and if they come by boat, our coast patrols
do their damnedest to ensure they never land.'
   A train grinds by, transparent as a fishbowl,
its passengers bright and separate, elsewhere-bound,
   who stare ahead. The wind is moaning cold.
A front door hanging slant like a flap of skin
bangs and bangs... Persephone sits waiting.

'There's one last site, a temple, we should visit –
   out at Sounion. Let's get started.'
And they drive. He finds her stern and forthright:
   the woman on the plane, a lie imparted
according to his known pre-requisites;
   a satin mask. *Among the dear departed,*
she shall reign: cruel, true, unwavering;
she carries out the curses of the living

upon the souls below and knows no anguish...
This rings inside his head like burning scripture.
Soon Athens' dish of radiance is eclipsed.
   The road winds up through trees, they park, and there –
a roofless columned hall upon a cliff,
   the sea beneath – a drop of sixty metres –
sighing on the stones. 'Lord Byron came
and in the marble chiselled out his name,

but to us this place is famous for Aegeus –
   father of Theseus, who forgot to change his sails
from black to white. Although he returned victorious
   from the labyrinth, his father thought he'd failed:
he glimpsed the ship and, frenzied with distress,
   jumped from the cliff and gave this sea its name.'
Donald surveys the wide and smooth Aegean,
the temple's broken tribute to Poseidon,

wind plucking at his coat and at his hair,
   and wonders why they're there. 'Since last year,
suicide in Greece has grown more popular –
   wives and daughters, sisters, nephews, brothers –
instances have doubled. Some favour here:
   it's desolate and high, without a barrier,
and, like Aegeus, they strew the sea beneath them
with what is left when all their hope is done.'

VI

And yet the wretched truth is this: Byron
   might summon a hero (however much he meant it)
to play the leading role in his *Don Juan*,
   to be seduced and fight; we cannot.
To be lucky both in war and amongst women
   in nineteenth-century Europe *could* have cut it
(even if, in Juan's case, it didn't) –
for royalty was useless (the hapless Regent),

untrammelled aristocracy in its cups,
   and the old bone-house of influence, glued
with noble blood, finally coming unstuck...
   One could be dashing, magnetic, brave, imbued
with rhetorical gifts and almost incredible luck
   and make things happen – a King's false pledge come true;
a fairer treaty drafted; a people freed.
One could be dramatic. God knows change was needed

and God knows change is also needed now –
   but the new bone-house of influence's been rebuilt
with corporations' cash; it won't allow
   outsiders to invade; it's defended to the hilt
and ruled by those with savvy media know-how.
   Governments bow to Businesses; Businesses sit
secure behind closed doors and ruminate
on how to best direct affairs of state.

We might run our story's *dénouement* as follows:
   like the scenes of Dickens' Ghost-of-Christmas-Present,
Persephone's display of Greece's sorrow
   works its full effect: Donald's incandescent.
He hurries back to Brussels, his soul aglow
   with a people's undeserved and cruel treatment
at the hands of the prosperous North... He barges in
on the Secretary's weekly Eurocrisis meeting,

demands an instant audience, *tête à tête*,
   and there unfurls a tale so sad, so shocking –
of a country where, if EU terms are met,
   everything goes to the dogs: law, policing,
the vestiges of a shredded welfare net
   to catch the unemployed and stop them starving –
the Secretary sighs. 'It's just as I suspected,'
he says when Donald's finished; 'It must be stopped' –

and while he's on the phone the camera switches
   to other phones which ring along the chain
in quick succession: a woman frowns, then flinches;
   a man listens, bangs his desk, then dials in turn
to his own boss higher up... And so, like stitches
   cast on one by one, what Donald's seen
accumulates its own materiality,
grows real and vivid, felt; and in the sanctity

of the EU's topmost echelons, in blood-wet gowns,
　　Austerity's merry surgeons down their scalpels.
Let's say we discover a brand-new Maynard Keynes:
　　a no-one up to now, a minor detail
in the ECB's machinery – good on loans
　　and fiscal policy generally – who has an apple-
moment, an insight, a hot Eureka!-flash
and proposes simply *giving* Greeks more cash,

to spend just as they like, side-stepping banks.
　　What would happen? The banjaxed wheels of commerce
could re-start; hand-outs be outflanked
　　by the sale of goods; an ever-increasing workforce
pay their taxes... Who forms a one-man think-tank,
　　which quickly grows and soon becomes the source
of *the* most radical EU plan in years:
a means for Greece to thrive without arrears

... But this is fancy. Donald wakes once more
　　in his muted room at nine the following morning.
She must have dropped him back; he can't remember.
　　His head is sore. The day is waiting –
a whole bright day to walk about without her –
　　and he's glad: her doleful talk of keening,
of savagery set loose and baited traps
has made him sick and might not quite be accurate –

Greece could shine completely differently
    in daytime. And he's starving. The breakfast's good
(yoghurt, honey, fruit and fried *haloumi*)
    and puts him in an optimistic mood,
fuelled by several cups of shot-gun coffee.
    He feels the way he usually does abroad:
inquisitive, free, undaunted, at his ease,
alert to pretty women (who aren't Persephone),

ready to explore. There's no museum staff,
    which means the great Acropolis is shut,
as is the home of Agamemnon's mask,
    of Santorini's frescoes, Nestor's cup...
But there are ships and islands. To Aegina perhaps?
    The ferry smokes, the anchor gets wound up,
Piraeus shrinks then falls off the horizon,
Donald inhales the salt of the churning ocean,

seagulls scream and dive in the ferry's wake,
    the winter sunlight's pale but trails its touch
abundantly, everywhere he looks,
    in the white waves' ruffled scrim, the masthead's torch.
He feels inside his pocket for his notebook,
    flicks it open. He hasn't written much:
'Athens', the date. Then, to be rid of her,
he adds her name and casts it on the water.

from ON BALANCE (2017)

THE MILLIHELEN

It never looks warm or properly daytime
in black-and-white photographs the sheer cliff-
face of the ship still enveloped in its scaffolding
backside against the launching cradle
ladies lining the quay in their layered drapery
touching their gloves to their lips and just as
They That Go Down to the Sea in Ships rises
from choirboys' mouths in wisps and snatches
and evil skitters off and looks askance
for now a switch is flicked at a distance
and the moment swollen with catgut-
about-to-snap with ice picks hawks' wings
pine needles eggshells bursts and it starts
grandstand of iron palace of rivets starts
moving starts slippery-sliding down
slow as a snail at first in its viscous passage
taking on slither and speed gathering in
the Atlas-capable weight of its own momentum
tonnage of grease beneath to get it waterborne
tallow soft soap train oil a rendered whale
this last the only Millihelen her beauty
slathered all over the slipway
faster than a boy with a ticket in his pocket
might run alongside it the bright sheet
of the Lough advancing faster than a tram
heavy chains and anchors kicking in
lest it outdoes itself straining up
to a riot of squeals and sparks lest it capsizes
before its beginning lest it drenches

the aldermen and the ship sits back in the sea
as though it were ordinary and wobbles
ever so slightly and then it and the sun-splashed
titled hills the railings the pin-striped awning
in fact everything regains its equilibrium.

ON BALANCE

May you be ordinary;
Have, like other women,
An average of talents:
Not ugly, not good-looking,
Nothing uncustomary
To pull you off your balance [...]
In fact, may you be dull

PHILIP LARKIN, 'BORN YESTERDAY'

Even fully grown,
she'd be a 'girl' to you.
You rarely mention women,
except to stress our looks
or what we cannot do,
though 'girls' persist
in separate, lit-up boxes –
their pants pulled down,
or getting fucked
by your luckier friend
in the toilet of a train.

You were the mean fairy
at the christening,
feigning honesty.
No doubt her father slapped
you on the back,
admired your dazzling
final turn from lack
to grudging benediction.
I wouldn't let you near
my brilliant daughter –

so far, in fact, from *dull,*
that *radiant, incandescent*
are as shadows on the landscape
after staring at the sun.

RECEIVING THE DEAD

for Jimmy McAleavey

I

Elementary, Watson,
    that the dead are legion,
eager to speak & awaiting
    a Wireless Telegraph
System to usher them in;
    that the pain of aeons
is galvanising… Bats chittering
    inside a cave's auditorium
or a thousand starlings
    amplifying evening over
the sodden docks: that sounds
    like this might issue forth
as soon as he flicks the switch
    should not be shocking –
receiver without transmitter,
    plugging itself into
the disturbed nest of the afterworld
    where everyone's still
at home, this amber lacquered box
    contains within its frame
the fits & shredded ectoplasm
    of our own dear century
in a twentieth-century form & bids
    all the dead welcome.
Listen –

A choir of fire –
   you are being watched
my little Friedel – the door jamb
   jammed & undulating,
the discarnate jostling for position
   at the microphone –
tell Daddy I'm – *the key's in your blue*
   coat pocket – *Selah* –
can't you remember? – giggles
   ascending their scales
then stopping, weeping, warnings –
   a war is – singing –
All She Gets from the Ice Man is Ice
   – whingeing –
you fucking knew I never meant to –
   Christ – diaphanous
acoustic entry point clogged
   & venomous, or worse,
tedious – *rain followed by snow* –
   let downs & come ons –
a baby who can't yet speak unleashing
   a caterwaul – instructions –
overhaul – *I'm sorry* not nearly as often
   as you'd think
& believe me more often.

3

To picture them, Watson,
 the only way we know how:
as Lazarus, say, pitched up
 on the other side for the second
time, in the coat of his own
 rot, but human, or the worst
of them pinned to their isolate
 stations, islands in a lake,
sheeted white & penancing,
 then hearing the click,
the chink made actual, the beckoning,
 to see them come running,
the boys & girls & men & women,
 their bare feet flashing –
is to err extravagantly. It must be.
 In the distances between
Signal Hill & Rathlin, between
 the curved horizon of Earth
& the ionosphere, they have become
 pure air, pure interruption –
a disturbance like a storm, further
 down the line, undressed
by electromagnetism. But wholly
 literate, they are equivalent
to language in its given state.

PLATINUM ANNIVERSARY

The two of us wound
into borrowed kimonos
on the temple steps

my heavy headgear
dagger tucked into my waist-
band should you ever

undress another
one flick of my ivory
wrist and I'd collapse

in the wet of my
small intestine my stomach
bridles soon enough

over uncooked eggs
at the airport and you you
star you crucible

my teeth are yours I
think my ribs removable
your unwavering

lantern frown above
my ice bed bloody sheets your
trousseau in my dream

I see our future
daughter driving a ragtop
and then I wake or

don't and there's this trick
your skin still does if I brush
my thumb along it

thronged notes spun into
one held hum by a gesture
all the hares lie down

and the two of us
just under half our lives and
this glitch we ride in

space together I
see precisely no one else
inside a shrinking

bubble of light the
minuscule part of matter
that's matter splitting

apart from itself
bright you singing on the stairway there's only you

NATIVITY

The assembly hall is full, though it's early still:
mums and dads on loan from their workaday offices;
littler brothers and sisters crashed out in pushchairs
and parked along the aisle like outsize baggage.
Chat rises up to perch among the rafters
and gets steadily amplified, making the walls resound.
Stewed tea in too-thin plastic scalds our hands.

And then it's dark and started. The Principal stands,
reminds us of the exits. He occupies his moment
so deliberately he might be chairing Congress.
And a decree went out. And all the boys and girls.
That all the world and several weeks' rehearsals
should be taxed. And thanks to those who helped
with sewing and thanks to those who witnessed

in their houses that a child was born this day
and thanks to everyone for turning up and time
to welcome the fixed astonishing star over Bethlehem
and all the other stars and please applause.
We turn as heliotropes to the sun to watch
a hundred preternaturally tiny children follow
their teachers in, and almost fail to recognise

our sons and daughters amongst them, so cleanly
have they been lifted from their context, so
splendidly have they been managing without us.
The chorus is dressed in red and green, the animals
in animal costumes, ten of them wear wings,
and here come the key anointed individuals –
the Virgin, the Husband, the Keeper, the Soldier –

they of transitive voices, survivors of many tests,
like Odysseus, whose reward is a human name
and, bar the two dear faces in the distance, backlit
with adoration, a room of strangers staring at them.
Narrators rise and fall to call the action points.
The songs break in as ponderous punctuation
and are exhausting for everyone. We half expect

the children to unhook themselves
from the strings of their teachers' attention
and to cry, or laugh, to scatter like birds off a lake,
but they don't, not now, not yet, and we are left
with a row of just-licked-by-a-cow-looking boys
in dressing gowns, Mary in a dress, Immanuel
in his cradle, low-key and ineffable, a portent

pointing the star of herself in two directions
at once, and this studded arena we've led them to,
these people whom we've forged, whose frankincense
we breathed when they were born, and we're sorry,
but we don't know how it happened, or what
the instructions are – we've left them in itchy
kneesocks, holding up a sign – or how it will end.

PERFUME

My Great Auntie Winnie may as well have spotted a crack
in the floor of Nottingham's Odeon Cinema –
beginning under the stage
like a telltale hairline fissure in a dam face
then zigzagging towards the exit –
as have been struck
by the actual bellwether that assailed her
the morning she trudged in to sweep and mop
and dust the flip-back seats
after the pop music concert the night before:
not just the common-enough stench of smoke
and sweat, but an extra still-warm
acrid musk, the mixed-in fug of a stable
in summer heat, hitting her like the reek
of a hospital laundry,
because in answer to *Love Me Do*, offered up
in spectacular harmony, two hundred
fourteen-year-old girls
had instantly wet themselves, screaming *Yes!*
We love you already!, but inaudibly,
each lone voice hopeless
against the squealing sheetmetal square of noise,
and so their bodies had taken over,
take this river, each shower a gift,
intimate and articulate, to whichever identikit member
they'd pinned their collapsing
stomachs on, each stream of steaming

yellow a flower, and as the crack grew ever wider
        and plaster flakes abandoned the ceiling
                and covered my Auntie's rollered
hair, she suddenly saw the street outside
        divide the length of the fissure, then the city,
                the north, the south, then all of England,
mothers on one side, daughters on the other,
        and the chasm between them strung
                with brilliant washing –
socks and vests and stockings and skirts and pants,
        rinsed clean with a bluebag in the kitchen sink,
                lifting in the wind.

12 FEBRUARY 1964

Picture it again
rope-throated by the scaffold
of scent so exquisite
to save him
their grannies serving them tea
Grew weirder
stacked along corridors
as if their children were scrofulous
or Jesus
had to stay so in tune
like slipping their arms
or balancing
They shredded
They auctioned off
Fans showed up
chambermaid uniforms
their car would be crawling
within seconds
shrieking to get
For all his dastardly
he went too far
on his wafted handkerchief
and so they unslippered him
out of love
They had to steal
like miscreants
bundled into
or fish vans
the boys they were
the Liverpool Lads
waving wildly
over

the hero at the end
unstoppers a bottle
the crowd pours round
It was weird from the beginning
on a saucer
Crutches & drips
mothers begging their touch
& they were Royalty Restored
They couldn't hear a thing
with one another
inside somebody else's sleeves
blindfolded
their hotel sheets
their knives & forks
in commandeered
If they left by the wrong exit
with women
faces of owls at the windscreen
let in
ravishment
whatever it was he unleashed
too much to bear
out of his skin
& ate him
from those seething stadiums
from a crime scene
laundry trucks
They left behind
as decoys
who cried to be famous
in the other direction
here

COLLIER

I

Though he never once placed a bet, my grandfather
sat in his chair every day and picked out winners:
Larkspur, League of Nations, Isinglass, Never Say Die

in the 2:30 at Epsom or Newmarket.
He'd follow their dips and peaks, ingesting the painfully
difficult newsprint on off-work afternoons,

or he'd rely on the tug-at-his-sleeve of instinct:
his grandmother's Romani nous with horses, his blacksmith-
father's apprising sense bred into his muscles and veins...

And so his damaged house filled up with winnings:
tickets to a race, pairs of boots to choose from,
a tea cosy from a shop, a pigeon cote out the back,

and after each spectacular nose-across-the-finish-line
outsider made him rich (which happened twice)
he'd sit and eat his wedding supper over again in his imagined

life: ham on the bone; salmon, roast beef, egg-and-cress; a cake.

2

No matter the shift, the only food he'd take with him
down the pit was bread and jam, two slices wrapped up
in greaseproof paper, and a bottle of gone-cold tea.

He'd perch in a cranny to eat it halfway through
his eight-hour stint at the coalface, black as a bat
bar the whites and reds of his eyes and his teeth's gapped ivory.

Each mine an auditorium. Under the fallen sun
of his headlamp, like the ghost of the boy he was
at the sorting station sorting out nuts from brights,

he'd array the sounds the tunnels carried
– the squeal of the wheel, an invisible neighbour's cough –
discarding each in turn until, in his blue-scarred palm,

he held up gold: miners' saviours in cages singing their lack
half a mile off, back by the fluted shaft, singing
no black damp, no gas, until he'd sing himself.

He knew eight-and-twenty ways to raise the roof, some safe, most not.

3

What possessed my granny, slim, smart, solvent, raising the roof
every Friday night after work at the Palais de Danse
in Nottingham, showing the band what-for with spies and soldiers,

to marry him? Some runaway freight car undid her, shunting her north.
Already his breath was a wounded animal pacing its ever-decreasing
circle underneath his rib cage. He couldn't afford linoleum.

The village had five shops. He was born in the reign of Victoria;
they'd finally buried the dead of Ypres just as my granny
came caterwauling in. Once, as a child,

visiting her spinster-aunt's friend in the countryside
who kept house for her younger brother, she was privy to this:
a walking shadow, the size and shape of a man,

stole across the room towards the kitchen, not touching anything.
The kettle's whistle. Splashing. Singing. Then the shut door
opened abruptly and out stepped a white vest and a clean face

and the moon's penumbra vanished into brightness.

4

Bright as a whitebell in Handley Wood, bright as the heads
of poor man's pepper shaking their throwaway lace
all over the lanes between New Whit and Eckington

was the evening he proposed (and the proud hart fleet
upon the enclosing hills and the honeycomb oozing honey).
And late the next day he stepped into a cage

and fell the length of a tarpitch mile, not looking, *yes*,
to where pit ponies stamped in their stalls, not listening, *yes*,
and was out along a by-line

dreaming his Skegness honeymoon into place
when a heaped tub of altogether coal, *yes you Tom Goodwin,
yes*, began snarling his name.

You might measure the force of its freak uncoupling
by what was crushed: it took an hour to manage the mess
of lungs and bones and blood to the surface.

He sat out in blankets and looked at the sea for his month at the Miners' Rest.

5

A month at a Miners' Rest, alright, but no compensation –
every time she paid a coal bill, or dressed my mother
in a cousin's pinafore, my granny would preen and peck

at the elderly man grown elderly early
hunched across from her in his armchair.
He'd turn himself into a tree and wouldn't answer.

And the silence of Glasshouse Lane burred with thistledown
like a blanket sewn by swallows just for them
would settle over the room

and he'd light up a woodbine and smile until she smiled too
and then the damp-blotched ceiling would open
and in their last companionable hours together

they'd play host to strange familiar visitors
soft-landing expertly in amongst the furniture:
Eric Coates *Calling All Workers*; Ralph Elman and his Bohemian Players;

Ron and Ethel taking forever to get nowhere in *Take It from Here*.

6

Because the distances you travel are unimaginable
to the man who flicks open each wing in a fan-card flourish
checking for balance and corkiness

before shunting you onto the train for your journey south
and over the freezing sea
towards liberation at Rheims or Poitiers

and because your tiny friable arrangement of magnets and air pockets
through which the planet articulates its cleverness
might be crushed by a falcon in an instant, but isn't,

and because your most exhilarating trajectory
is not just from darkness to light, as his is,
but from darkness to the upper storeys of the air itself –

coaxing you down off the toss from Bordeaux or Nantes
to the landing board, getting your leg-ring clocked,
is to stand with a capful of coins in the Miners' Arms, a balloon
                                                            adventurer,

or like a man who has tasted the rind of the moon, without ever leaving
                                                            home.

THE MAYFLY
i.m. Lilian Bland, 1878–1971

Conspicuously mis-christened – what chink
in the general atmosphere, what sudden
lift of bones and breath

allowed you to stand up straight in mechanic's overalls
(*skirts are out of the question*) and plot
your escape route into the sky?

Like the right foot of Louis Blériot,
trapped beside one of his overheating
engines, like the umpteen previous

biplane extravaganzas that had left the ground
– *gadzooks!* – for a couple of minutes
only to wobble uncontrollably

in recalcitrant space and then nosedive,
everything flared white hot
for you until it abruptly ended:

jujutsu, shooting, horseracing,
spending days on remote Scottish
islands photographing seabirds.

You donned your Donegal cap
(*the natives, I hear, thought one of the mills
had blown up but put it down*

to a thunderstorm) and tapped your cigarette ash
all over Edwardian decorum;
if Blériot wouldn't let you near

                    his Channel-hopping aeroplane –
                        you'd begged him in a letter
                            to crown you as his passenger –

you'd build and fly your own.
        The unflexed, held-aloft wingspan
            of gulls in flight was where you started,

            in the Tobercorran workshop,
                your gardener's-son assistant
                    holding your tools and worshipping

                you from a distance. *I enclose*
                    two photos of my biplane,
                        the 'Mayfly'; she is the first

biplane to be made in Ireland:
        skids of ash, ribs and stanchions
            of spruce, bamboo outriggers

            taut beneath unbleached calico,
                more grasshopper than aircraft.
                    You ran the finished may-fly,

                may-not fly still missing its engine
                    and airy as a climbing frame off the top
                        of Carnmoney Hill,

Belfast smouldering under its furnaces,
        the Lough a phlegmatic eye,
            casually watching, and hung

as a counterweight four six-foot
          volunteers from the Irish Constabulary
          who saw the ground ripped clear

          of their feet in an upward gust
               and were trailed alarmingly over
                    heads of astonished livestock

before dropping off.
     In the movie of your life
          they haven't scripted yet

          all bets are on from this moment
               (*it is quite a new sensation being charged*
               by an aeroplane) –

          a horizontally opposed two-cylinder
               engine with the help of a whiskey
                    bottle and an ear trumpet

gets fitted next and Lord O'Neill
     of Randalstown Park, so struck
     by your exploits, offers up

          his level acreage as a refuge
          and launching point.
               (*The engine is beautifully balanced*

but all the same the vibration
is enormous ... the nuts
dance themselves loose.)

Hooked all your life on barter –
    a glider for an aeroplane, an aeroplane
        for a motorcar, England

            for Ireland, Ireland
                for Canada – you knew this was
                    the single most inflammable

                        exchange you'd ever risk, the lone bull
                            standing slack under hawthorn
                                at the edge of the field,

quick chatter-and-flash
    from the hedgerow,
        enough of a canopy of willowy light

            to finally allow admittance,
                and saw, as you climbed up
                    to your tilted seat and got

                        those improbable Victorian pram wheels
                            started, a straggle of farmhands
                                and scullery maids,

politely assembled, all wishing you
    skywards. Once it was finished,
        you ran back, over and over,

to the proof it had happened: the tracks
of her passage in the spangled grass,
and then their absence –

your footprint missing on earth for the span
of a furlong, as if a giant had lifted its boot
and then set it down.

MY LIFE ACCORDING TO YOU

So I was born and was small for ages
and then suddenly a cardboard box
appeared with two furry black ears
sticking out of it it made me nervous
but I was brave and gave it a bell
to play with and then out it jumped
and loved me it was my cat I called it
Morris Morrissey it matched
my mother's Morris Minor

                    For the next bit

I was a teenager and then I grew up
I had a flat in Dublin and a boyfriend
he was a vet little bed little kitchen
little towel rack lots of little cups
and saucers and then off he went
to Africa he sent me pictures
of giraffes and of the second
tallest waterfall in the world
when he got back he wasn't my friend

                    anymore I cried

for a week I was also at university
a bigger place than school with bigger
chairs and desks and when it finished
I found a suitcase it was red
with purple flowers it had a scarf
around the handle I put in everything
I needed socks and a jotter and snacks
and took a plane across the ocean
to Japan to visit Godzilla

                                    where it was

summer and boiling hot and the people
all kept wind chimes to make it
cooler and rode bicycles to the shops
and at the same time held up umbrellas
though it wasn't even raining
and when I met a man in a bright
white classroom the darkest parts
of our eyes turned into swirls then question
marks then hearts so we got married

                              and went hippety

hoppety splat a mountain a lake
a desert we bought a house a tiny one
at first and then a massive one a baby
knocked at the door one night
but didn't come in and then another
baby came he cried a lot
we thought he had a tummy ache
we gave him a bath in a bucket
he was just lonely

                              for his sister

to come and keep him company
but you were still floating about
in space inside your bubble egg
it had accessories a switch
for going sideways a switch
for going upside down or faster
it was a cross between a sparkly green
and a sparkly silver the moon
was very annoying and then whenever

                              we'd all been bored

on our own for long enough down
you came on a path of lightning
to finish off the family you were born
on the living room floor at three
in the morning in front of the trampoline-
sofa and I heard them say *A Girl!*
and sat up straightaway we were both
pretty and I opened out my arms
and that's it really

When you grow up

I'm going to be *so* busy taking you
to the house shop waiting by the playground gates to bring your children
swimming I won't be any different
I'll keep your room exactly as it is
for you to visit bric-a-brac collection
on the shelf the bed your father built
the letters of your name in neon
appearing on the ceiling

                    when it's time

ARTICULATION

And these, ladies and gentlemen, are the bones
of Napoleon's horse, Marengo. Articulated thus
– tibia to fibula, scapula to humerus,
appendicular skeleton latched to the dome
of the spine and the thin ribs' hanging flaps
encasing the space of the missing heart --
he seems refashioned out of a craft kit,
a balsawood model everyhorse, perhaps.
I am looking at eyes that looked at the Emperor
is nothing, however, to this: neither a coffee pot
nor toothbrush, nor His finest pearl-grey coat
from the mausoleum; not plaster
squeezed into the shape of what's been lost
to bring it back to life as a death mask,
a punched-through backwards photograph
of itself; nor any of the things embossed
by use or touch or freer association
(loose talk, hearsay) with His shining likeness –
these very hooves trod mud at Austerlitz,
this very sacrum made final victory certain.
Moreover, put your eye to the eye socket
(one by one and gently) and observe
what changes: your straight perspective curves,
the floor on which you're standing tilts,
the room's clear atmosphere thickens
and as mirrors angled off against each other
produce an endless vaulted corridor
to somewhere else, still truer things are given:
of-all-the-Russias snow, a sky of smoke,
the bite of iron, entrails in a heap,
curled up like an outgrown foal, a man asleep

inside a horse's ruptured stomach ...
That's how close Marengo stands to history –
Sphenoid, Vomer, Lacrimal, Mandible –
for however long he lasts before he crumbles,
portal, time machine, skeleton key
to what cannot be imagined. Who could resist
a ticket to the steaming blooded fields
of Europe just as the dog star fades?
Hold your breath now while I show you this.

DAS DING AN SICH
East Prussia, January 1945

a pig   two cows   a dray horse   geese
by the back door   gaggle of grandmothers
kiln-dry barns   hay until summer
gardens tucked into an orderly slumber

cutlery stewpots   teakettles   delft
eggs in a blue bowl   buttercheesehamhockmilk
tables scrubbed clean as a wishbone
spliced hares hanging from hooks   sickle-fat

wireless   gramophone   grandfather clock
a reading lamp   a newspaper rack
dead sons like icons   on the wall   *Wehrmacht*
collars starched stiff   a sewing basket

lavender bags   June stowed between folds
in a blanket chest   bed sheets   bath towels
patchwork quilts   cupboards of petticoats
nightgowns   lace   & afterwards

such ransacked   pillows
such bayoneted   eiderdowns
a white-out of feathers   in bedrooms
hallways alleyways courtyards squares

like after-Christmas snow   or nouns
unmoored   from speech
in the blistering static   of *Grossdeutscher*
Rundfunk's   final broadcast

Because of so much colour – purples greens and blues, yellow, copper, reds –
where we least expect it, Prokúdin Gorsky's outpost villagers seem more like us
dressed up than like themselves, posing in a past bequeathed to them in snatches
rather than interrupted from the task at hand. The girls look mismatched,
overfitted, stuffed into what was left after the travelling theatre's costume box
got ransacked. Old at seven, elbows out and serious as tax inspectors,
in layered skirts so beetroot they could have been soaked in soup,
these three proffer china plates of forest berries in variegated shades –
iris, magenta, plum – which ricochet in turn as a kind of rhyme
off floral handkerchiefs, pleated aprons, blouses, cuffs
dipped in dyes we haven't seen the like of. They can't be comfortable –
or are they merely wilful, staying put on the wrong side of the century,
refusing to wear trousers? The cerise shirt on the back of the man
in the open-shaft iron mine, resting on his shovel, the barge haulers,
woodcutters and troops of riverboatmen in vests the colour of duck eggs
turn 'Volga Work Parties 1905' into a room next door we might briefly visit
where nothing would surprise us. Want to see my boots? asks a foreman,
tipping up one foot at a cocky angle. The headscarf on his wife ignites a meadow.
And if, because they're richer, living in a town, or in thrall to Queen Victoria

and her calamitous black, some people have fought back their spectral natures,
choosing instead to appear to us both looped-at-the-waist and dark, the buildings
behind them haven't: whole streets rise seashell pink or powder blue
out of the middle picture, ringing the radical bells of themselves for miles around.
Over *Goloднaya Stiep*, or Starving Steppe, the weather cooperates also:
this sky exactly half of what's been taken two shades brighter than lazuli
with no rain cloud in sight is as good as God's promise to Ishmael
for the women scything a hayfield underneath it. Tashkent, Archangel, Samarkand.
Here he's stopped for a moment en route (these days his perpetual state)
for a rare self-portrait: hatted, moustachioed, bespectacled, thin,
Chief Photographer to the Tsar. You can tell he's already distracted
by the thought of his railway-car darkroom, a gift from Nicholas himself,
where the three magic filters for his new magic lantern will approximate what was there.
This particular Babushka on this particular veranda on this particular evening
in this particular summer is spinning a skein of wool. Tomorrow night is bath night.
In the morning, she'll step out of the clothes she owns including her footcloths
and into her second shift, boil a copper of water, slosh and sluice them clean
with a stick of birch, then hang them out to dry all day, like the flags
of a continent's countries strung across her garden, so that afterwards,
her hair de-gritted and every pore alive, not a single unwashed item touches her skin.

THE SINGING GATES

Up on top of Divis on a freezing Saturday
we pass the singing gates: five five-barred silver yokes

across from the café (closed for renovation),
penning nothing in but their own frustration.

They keen like washerwomen into the billowing sky.
You're talking Batman, Two-Face, Robin; you lope

ahead and circle and run back, ready to walk
for hours if we have time, free at last of school

and all the worksheets you never manage to finish
on your own. I can no longer ask my grandad

exactly how his release was managed back in April
'45: five years of his young man's life wiped out

for being a so-called Enemy of the State in wartime
(that other bout of internment no one ever mentions)

and then what? Tipped out onto the pavement like a sack
of damaged apples as the gates of Crumlin Road Gaol

clanged shut behind him? My father says he walked
to this summit the very next morning, walked

to work every day thereafter, walked to think,
walked for pleasure, walked to stretch each inch of his cell

by laying it down, over and over, on the floor
of the borderless world, so that its chipped-tile cast-iron

rectangle could disappear ... We opt for the Ridge Trail,
a heathery zigzag that wraps the whole side of the hill

in its ribbon, while the Joker secedes to mummification
and the death rites of Ancient Egypt. You're a dark-haired

flurry in a hailstorm, running on sugar and bliss,
who can't tell *b* from *d* because *any* letter might just flick

its Fred Astaire hat and dance backwards across the page
if it felt like it, yet starving all the same for knowledge –

imbibing the French Revolution or species of cacti
like brawn and remembering everything.

My grandad brought his own son here from the age of four
on crippling, all-day hikes on Saturdays

(long before, as the Jesuits saw it, my father had the capacity
for resistance to anything) and told him brilliant stories:

the Battle of Stalingrad, the Defence of the Luding Bridge,
The Great Only Appear Great Because We Are on Our Knees,

Let Us Rise – until the two of them fell asleep
in Hatchet Field, clouds passing over their faces like zeppelins.

The oil rigs you fell in love with a year ago
are still moored at the shipyard's glittering edge.

Storms of gunmetal grey touch down precisely in far-off
tinkertoy villages though for now we're walking in sunshine,

welcome as any downpour after a drought, as you list
the typical contents of a sarcophagus and detail the risk

of double jeopardy in the Hall of Two Truths –
Did you bring joy? Did you find joy? –

Horus skulking hawk-eyed in the background.
For most of my father's childhood, his father must have looked

like the man in the black-and-white photograph I keep sequestered
in a notebook: a Guest of Honour in the Soviet Union, turned Italian

in the Black Sea sunshine, his hallmark Donegal suit
dramatically cut, skinny like you and even more electric,

a honey magnet (and he knew it) for secretaries, receptionists,
stray passing female fellow revolutionaries

in that dim hermetic time lock called Transport House
with its tea trolleys, telephone exchanges,

ash trays standing guard along corridors
like Russian Babushkas in apartment blocks.

We can pick out its derelict white-black-and-turquoise
(Belfast's only example of Socialist Realist architecture)

from the rest of the city centre's humdrum colours.
Do you want to ask me a question, Mummy?

(by far your favourite question) as we come up at last
by our circuitous route to the granite triangulation point

where, three months earlier, my granddad's children
and their children and their children took turns with a kitchen scoop

to launch what was left of him into the air.
He'd made himself so small in the previous months,

perhaps out of courtesy, it hadn't been hard
and I want to ask you about the gates

we're on our way back to – what wind caught where?
In what cavity? Why this particular calibre of sound

unravelling only here? Are they in harmony? Are they a choir?
Are they, in fact, the singing ticket to the afterlife

and how might we post ourselves into it, limb by limb?
What scarab? What amulet? What feather? What scale? What spell?

WHITELESSNESS

I

The Geologist

The rocks on Greenland are the oldest on Earth.
This one's a fossilised algal mat; this one
contains the ridges of human teeth:
some early Palaeolithic adolescent caught
grinning at the moment of death
in a stone photograph. We manoeuvre
them down to the beach on a stretcher.
Ochres and greys and blacks
ricochet back and forth across the massif,
as denuded of white as the West of Ireland,
while the shed ice bobs in the bay
begging smaller and smaller comparisons –
lozenges dissolving visibly on the tongue;
droplets of fat on broth. *If it's life*
that controls the geological machinery
of the planet, rather than the other way round,
we are neither new, nor tragic. This came
to me one morning as I sorted out my cabin
and the hundreds of marathon runners
in my brain stopped and changed direction.

2

The Photographer

The world speaks to me through signs.
Tiny signs. Missable signs. The stones
in the river are speaking to me.
How many decades has this ox skull lain here?
It looks like a crime scene. A waterfall
rises as mist off the face of the rock,
missing its ending. The red earth holds up
a rainbow on its outstretched hands.
We sailed right to the edge of a glacier
in a dinghy yesterday, pushed
against it, hard, but it didn't budge
or squeal. It was the colour
of desert turquoise and implacable.
When we got back, I made a map
of my life, with holes for hideouts
between birth and death, and showed it
to my friend. In the beginning,
God put a rainbow in the sky
as a promise
that He'd never let the ocean rise again.

3

The Geographer

IKKE OPMÅLT says the map: unexplored.
– *What's this valley called?*
– *What would you like to call it?*
For the first few days we practise
with rifles on the pebbly beach,
though it's hardly dangerous:
polar bears are visible for miles
against the darker hillsides. Bog cotton
nods in swathes above the permafrost.
Lars and Simon buzz about the sky
in their flying dinghy, taking aerial
photographs, while we concentrate
on drilling up the planet's large intestine
and seeing what it's eaten. Ridiculously
overdressed, two musk ox trundle past.
We must sound enormous –
where before there were only kittiwakes,
the occasional seaward explosion
of an iceberg disintegrating –
but they blank us nevertheless.

4

The Artist

I packed Anthrax,
Megadeth, Metallica. I packed
two dozen sketchpads and sixteen
boxes of pencils. Shell's Arctic exploratory
outriders in their magenta lifejackets
can kiss my shiny metal ass.
I did not pack colours. Our foremast
resembles a crucifix. I stuck my boot
on the skull of an ox as though I'd shot it
and smiled at the camera. *Running / On our way*
hiding / You will pay dying / One thousand deaths…
I straddle the prow of the ship to sketch
whatever it is I'm looking at
and the daylight lasts and lasts.
For all the white animals – the hares,
the foxes, the wolves – I just leave
spaces on the paper where their bodies were
last time I glanced up. The rest
I filibuster in in grey or black
to stop the quiet.

5

The Marine Biologist

FUCK EVERYTHING BECOME A PIRATE
declares my t-shirt, but I don't mean it.
Ocean invertebrates are inconceivably lovely.
Each morning, I lower a bucket over
the side of the ship, clank it back up
on deck, then stick my hand
inside the sea's feely bag. In countless
numbers, the fjord system's summer whales
perform their languid acrobatics
within metres of the bowsprit.
Transfer even a soupçon of meltwater
to a Petri dish and, hush, the world's
most previously inaccessible ballet-
dancers are practising arabesques.
Such secretly parted curtains!
Last Friday I identified
an entirely new species of Annelid,
a male and a female, framed
and translucid under the microscope's hood:
they appeared to be having sex.

6

The Archaeologist

Uncover a single nick on a flint
made to sharpen it and you've nailed it:
the Paleo-Eskimo village –
which must have existed
here, where this gneiss is –
hoves into view: their Big Tent
(open to the sea); their Stone Age
playground. Laughter. Dogs. Fire.
Then nothing for three hundred
thousand years and now me, in my Ushanka.
The fact was he'd gone looking for his father.
Lower down the coast, we stood
on the deck of the ship
and watched a polar bear
attacking an outpost. Then
we went to look. It had shredded
the pages of a *Reader's Digest.*
Before we got there, its long body had lolloped
away over the rocks and, even from a distance,
had kept on flashing back at us, like Morse.

VERY DYSPRAXIC CHILD

Foiled – and not for the first time –
by a timewarp villain, who sports a monocle
and a Hitler Youth haircut, who drones
about the sky in a Flying Baron
plotting his secret green riotous tectonics,
Batman – bewildered, back-footed, bilious,
shaking that metal-wedge chin of his and drooping
in the puddle of his own dejection – Batman
changes tack, hurtles deep inside the cave of his Bat
Resources and flaps out sneakily immune
to the expanding circles of dizziness that loop
the room and everyone in it in a ship's sick tilt,
emanating from the dastardly eye piece, yes,
Batman's practised crossing the mid-line
a zillion times a day, his elbows flashing
so fast they make blurry triangles, his eyes
obediently ricocheting to their corners,
inducing an ice-cream headache, Batman's
walked over the wobbly bridge of his inner
playground all the way to the end and so what
if the children stared and pointed, so what
if it took so long the sun went down
and even the moon made fun of him
with its o*h–but–the–tedium* 'O', the next time
some malefactor buckles the floor
in front of him into jagged peaks and troughs,
laughing like a maniac, or pitches a ball
at his face he hasn't been able to catch,
or urges him, sarcastically, to get on his bike
and be free – free of the ill-set, bifurcated shackles
that pin him to himself – he'll be ready:

echolocation's the least
of his snazzily packed weapons of defence
and Batman Resurrected isn't the adversary
you'd assumed you'd be dealing with, is he, in fact
you may as well order those shipping crates
lowered now, kiss goodbye
to the twenty-four-carat diamond watches
snug in their velvet cases, the bullion bars,
and come out holding your hands up, Dr Vertigo.

THE ROPE

I have paused in the door jamb's shadow to watch you
          playing Shop or Cliff! or Café or Under-the-Sea
among the flotsam of props on our tarmacked driveway.
          All courtship. All courtesy.

At eight and six, you have discovered yourselves friends,
          at last, and this the surprise the summer
has gifted me, as if some
          penny-cum-handkerchief conjuror

had let loose a kingfisher…
          You whirl and pirouette, as in a ballet,
take decorous turns, and pay for whatever you need
          with a witch's currency:

grass cuttings, sea glass, coal, an archaeopteryx
          of glued kindling from the fire basket;
you don two invisible outsize overcoats – for love?
          for luck? – and jump with your eyes shut.

And I can almost see it thicken between you,
          your sibling-tetheredness, an umbilicus,
fattened on mornings like this as on a mother's blood,
          loose, translucent, not yet in focus,

but incipient as yeast and already strong enough
          to knock both of you off your balance
when you least expect it, some afternoon after work,
          decades hence,

one call from a far-flung city and, look,
      all variegated possibles – lovers, kids, apartments –
whiten into mist; the rope is flexing,
      tugging you close and you come, obedient

children that you are, back to this moment,
      staggering to a halt and then straightening,
grown little again inside your oversize coats and shoes
      and with sea glass still to arrange, but without me watching.

from THE BOOK OF KNOWLEDGE OF
INGENIOUS MECHANICAL DEVICES

Just as the world to Al-Jazari
was a wonder of *tawhid,*
all visible things

the über-florid signature of God,
so is his book
a wonder of understanding

of what can be borne up
and what will topple
given gravity, air pressure,

time, which is itself encased
in stunning script: Baikal
poured into a single

shell or glass receptacle.
Inventor of such leaps
in engineering

as the camshaft, crankshaft,
throttling valve,
the calibration of orifices

and the balancing
of static wheels – theophanies
that awed all Anatolia,

upon which our modernday
buoyancy depends –
he was also fanciful, elaborate,

absurd, who made water
issue from the fountainhead
in the shape of a shield

or like a lily-of-the-valley.
Flick open his pages
and listen to the clicking

of dismantled
humanoid automata
reconstructing themselves

from the bottom
up, then stepping back
from the task accomplished:

a towel proffered, a wine cup
filled, the victim
of phlebotomy distracted.

Close over the flyleaf
and watch what fades:
enamel the colour

of a peacock feather,
roundels, falcons,
anklets, diadems, bells –

fripperies
of fine technology
he stacked in Saladin's

palace workshop
solely for themselves –
which is like waking slowly

of your own accord,
the dream world oddly
tilted at your feet

for ages, for a year,
until it almost vanishes,
leaving the ghosted

impress of its ardour
still folded
in the bedclothes.

'Flight'
I am indebted here to Michael McKeon's *The Origins of the English Novel, 1600-174* (John Hopkins University Press, 1987), which first brought the 'miraculous' flight of Charles II in 1651 to my attention. Other details in the poem are taken from Samuel Pepys' *His Majesty Preserved: An Encounter of King Charles II's Escape After the Battle of Worcester*, first published in 1680 (Falcon Press, 1954).

'Vanity Fair'
This poem is inspired by William Makepeace Thackeray's novel *Vanity Fair* (1847–48), in which the widow Amelia Osbourne (née Sedley) writes a letter to her long-term admirer William Dobbin, after he has finally despaired of winning her love and left her. Because the contents of the letter are not described by Thackeray, I have attempted to fill in what he left out.

'York'
This is a found poem drawn from the contents list of the *York Mystery Plays* (Oxford World Classics, 2009). 'And episodes in between with a yet more fabulous cohabiting', and the two final lines, are my own.

'1801'
This poem is an imaginative re-voicing of Dorothy Wordsworth inspired by *The Grasmere Journals, 1800-1803* (Oxford University Press, 1991).

'Jigsaw'
At the centre of this poem is the world's first jigsaw puzzle: a
map of Europe entitled 'Europe Divided into its Kingdoms'
(1766) by London cartographer John Spilsbury.

'Puzzle'
See Boris A. Kordemsky's *The Moscow Puzzles: 359
Mathematical Recreations* (Penguin, 1972).

'Photographing Lowry's House'
I imagine the speaker of this poem to be Denis Thorpe, a
photographer for the *Guardian* who gained access to Lowry's
home just after the painter had died.

'A Matter of Life and Death'
This poem draws heavily on the British film of the same title by
Michael Powell and Emeric Pressburger released in the Britain
in 1946 and in the United States as *Stairway to Heaven* in 1947.

'The Doctors'
See David King, *The Commissar Vanishes: The Falsification of
Photographs and Art in Stalin's Russia*, (Metropolitan Books,
1997).

'The Millihelen'
A *millihelen* is a fanciful unit of measurement used to describe
'the amount of physical beauty required to launch a single ship'.
This poem revisits the *Titanic*'s successful launch into the waters
of Belfast Lough in 1911.

'Receiving the Dead'
When Guglielmo Marconi invented the radio in 1898, he was
convinced that this new technology was the perfect medium for
picking up the voices of the dead. Thomas Edison and Nikola

Tesla were two other famous believers in Electronic Voice Phenomena (EVP).

'Perfume'
The second part of this poem incorporates the final scene of Patrick Süskind's novel *Perfume: The Story of a Murderer* (Penguin Essentials, 2010).

'Collier'
This poem recounts the life of my maternal grandfather Tom Goodwin (1898-1966). Of Roma heritage, he worked as a coalminer in the North Derbyshire/South Yorkshire coalfields before being injured in a mining accident for which he was never compensated.

'The Mayfly'
In 1910, Lilian Bland, who lived in Carnmoney, County Antrim, became the first woman in the world to design, build and fly her own aeroplane.

'Articulation'
Napoleon's horse, Marengo, was captured as a victory trophy during the Battle of Waterloo and taken to England, where he later died. His reconstructed skeleton is part of the collection of the National Army Museum, Chelsea. 'I am looking at eyes that looked at the Emperor' is a quotation from *Camera Lucida: Reflections on Photography* (Vintage: 2000) by Roland Barthes.

'The Singing Gates'
This poem is a homage to my paternal grandfather Sean Morrissey (1921-2016), who was interned during the Second World War as a suspected IRA activist. Later he 'converted' to Communism, travelling on several occasions to the Soviet Union, and worked as the Education Officer for the Transport and

General Workers' Union in Transport House in Belfast.

'Whitelessness'
This poem is inspired by the documentary *Expedition to the End of the World* by Daniel Dencik, first released in Denmark in 2013.

'From *The Book of Knowledge of Ingenious Mechanical Devices*'
The Book of Knowledge of Ingenious Mechanical Devices (1206) is an early masterwork on mechanical engineering written by Ismail-al-Jazari. *Tawhid* is an Arabic term meaning the oneness of God. The lines in italics are taken from *The Book of Ingenious Devices* (850), a source of inspiration for the later text.

ACKNOWLEDGEMENTS

My sincere thanks to Michael Schmidt and all the team at
Carcanet for their work on my six poetry collections to date over
the course of the last quarter-century.

I would like to thank Jonathan Galassi of Farrar, Straus &
Giroux (New York) for publishing *Parallax and Selected Poems* in
the USA in 2015.

Thanks are also due to the editors of the following publications
in which some of these poems, or versions of them, have
previously appeared:

> *An Anthology of Modern Irish Poetry* (Belknap Press of
> Harvard University, 2010), *The Antioch Review, Archipelago,
> Atlanta Review, Being Alive* (Bloodaxe, 2004), *The Cincinnati
> Review, Eavan Boland: Inside History* (Arlen House, 2017),
> *Edinburgh Review, A Fine Statement* (Poolbeg Press, 2008),
> *Female Lines: New Writing by Women from Northern Ireland*
> (New Island Books, 2017), *fermata: Writings Inspired by Music*
> (Artisan House, 2016), *The Forward Book of Poetry* (2006,
> 2010, 2011, 2018), *The Guardian, Hwaet! 20 Years of Ledbury
> Poetry Festival* (Bloodaxe, 2016), *Identity Parade: New British
> and Irish Poets* (Bloodaxe, 2010), *The Independent on Sunday,
> Irish Pages, Love Poet, Carpenter: Michael Longley at Seventy*
> (Enitharmon Press, 2010), *Making for Planet Alice* (Bloodaxe,
> 1997), *Metre, Modern Women Poets* (Bloodaxe, 2005), *The
> Moth, New Hibernia Review, The New Irish Poets* (Bloodaxe,
> 2004), *The New North: Contemporary Poetry from Northern*

Ireland (Salt, 2011), *New Poetries II* (Carcanet, 1999), *New Walk, New Welsh Review, The Penguin Book of Irish Poetry* (Penguin Classics, 2010), *Poems of the Decade: An Anthology of the Forward Books of Poetry* (2011), *PN Review, Poetry, Poetry Daily, Poetry Ireland Review, Poetry London, The Poetry Review, Southword, The Stinging Fly, Subtropics, The Wake Forest Book of Irish Women's Poetry* (Wake Forest University Press, 2011), *The Wake Forest Series of Irish Poetry Volume I* (Wake Forest University Press, 2004), *The Well Review* and *The Yellow Nib.*

'1801' was a Poem on the Underground in February 2018.

'China' was commissioned by the British Council as part of the Writers' Train China Project in 2003.

'*Don Juan, 2012*' was commissioned by Andy Croft and N.S. Thompson and published in *A Modern Don Juan: Cantos for These Times by Divers Hands* (Five Leaves, 2014).

'Collier' was commissioned by the Durham Book Festival as part of the Festival Laureateship in 2015.

Thanks are also due to the Arts Council of Northern Ireland/ Heritage Lottery for a Major Artist Individual Award in 2012, and to Château de Lavigny, Switzerland, for a residency in 2009.

INDEX OF POEM TITLES